BUSINESS PRICING AND INFLATION

This book probes some of the theoretical and empirical aspects of inflation, focusing particularly on the determination of changes in output prices. It argues that the causes of inflation should be discussed within a framework which incorporates conflict over income shares. Firms aim for increases in profits, and workers for increases in real wages, and there is no strong reason to think that those increased claims are compatible. It is important also to discuss inflation in the context of a "credit money" economy, where banks loans and trade credit usually expand in line with increased demand for credit to finance higher expenditure, whether it arises from higher prices or higher outputs. This book places much emphasis on the distinction between competitive theories of pricing which stress the role of excess demand and expectations and the wide variety of theories of pricing and of firm behavior which can be summarized in terms of price seen as a mark-up over costs. About half of the book is concerned with empirical work relevant to these issues, and draws heavily on an investigation by the author and his collaborators into pricing behavior in British manufacturing industries over the period 1963 to 1975. After a review of the difficulties of testing excess demand theories, it presents much evidence which points to the empirical invalidity of this approach, and which has important implications for the monetarist approach to macroeconomics often built on the excess demand view. The examination of the mark-up approach to pricing generates support for that general approach, and indicates that changes in demand pressures and in labor costs are of little importance in the determination of price changes. The empirical work also illustrates substantial differences in pricing behavior between industries, and thus casts doubt on an aggregative approach to price determination.

Malcolm C. Sawyer is Reader in Economics at the University of York. He was previously Lecturer in Economics at University College London. His other books are listed on the next page.

Also by Malcolm C. Sawyer

MACRO-ECONOMICS IN QUESTION
ECONOMICS OF INDUSTRIES AND FIRMS
THEORIES OF THE FIRM
BIG BUSINESS (*with Sam Aaronovitch*)

BUSINESS PRICING AND INFLATION

Malcolm C. Sawyer

in collaboration with Sam Aaronovitch and
Peter Samson

St. Martin's Press   New York

Library of Congress Cataloging in Publication Data

Sawyer, Malcolm C.
Business pricing and inflation.

Bibliography: p.
Includes index.
1. Inflation (finance)   2. Price policy.   3. Price
policy—Great Britain.   I. Aaronovitch, Sam.
II. Samson, Peter.   III. Title.
HG229.S297   1983   332.4'1   83-3121
ISBN 0-312-10908-3

Contents

List of Figures

List of Tables

Preface

This book originated in a research project undertaken by Sam Aaronovitch and myself on price behaviour in British manufacturing industry over the period 1963 to 1975. In the early part of the project we were assisted by Sadick Johaadien who collected much of the data used. Peter Samson, as research associate, assembled further data, and undertook much of the vast amount of econometric estimation involved. He also contributed much to the general development of the research programme.

The ideas expressed in this book were subject to much discussion between Sam Aaronovitch, Peter Samson and myself, and in that sense this book represents the joint work of the three of us. It was decided, however, that in light of our current interests and activities that I should take responsibility for writing up the results of our research programme in the form of a book. The inputs of the other two are acknowledged by the inclusion of their names on the title-page. But, whilst they agree with the broad thrust of what is written, they do not necessarily agree in every detail.

We are grateful to the Social Science Research Council for financial support (under grant no. HR 4921/2) which enabled Peter Samson to be employed for two years as a research associate. I am grateful to Basil Blackwell Publishers Ltd, for permission to draw extensively on the joint paper with Sam Aaronovitch entitled "Price Change and Oligopoly" which appeared in the *Journal of Industrial Economics*, vol. 30, and to Chapman and Hall Ltd, for permission to draw extensively on the joint paper with Sam Aaronovitch and Peter Samson entitled "The Influence of Cost and Demand Changes on the Rate of Change of Prices" which appeared in *Applied Economics*, vol. 14.

M.C.S.

1 Inflation, Pricing and Profits

INTRODUCTION

In recent years inflation has often been presented as a major, if not *the* major economic problem facing many industrialised capitalist countries. During the 1970s, the rate of price inflation averaged an annual rate of over 13 per cent in the UK, nearly 8 per cent in the USA and 9 per cent in the OECD area as a whole. These rates of inflation were considerably above those experienced in the 1950s and 1960s, when the typical rates of inflation were more like 2 to 4 per cent per annum. Governments often appeared to be evicted from office through a failure to control or reduce inflation, whilst others were elected on the promise of controlling inflation. Increasingly, Western governments have pursued restrictive fiscal and monetary policies, with the declared aim of the reduction of the rate of inflation. Judged by the results in terms of inflation, these policies have been singularly unsuccessful, with at the time of writing, the lowest rate of inflation in the UK since 1973 being 9 per cent (in 1978) and 5.8 per cent in the USA. Alongside these deflationary policies, unemployment has been high and rising. In the United Kingdom it has been above 5 per cent of the labour force since 1975, and had reached 14 per cent by mid-1982. In the United States with unemployment statistics derived in a different manner, unemployment has remained generally above 6 per cent. Across the OECD area, unemployment averaged under $3\frac{1}{2}$ per cent in the first five years of the 1970s, rose to nearly $5\frac{1}{4}$ per cent in the second five years and then to nearly 6 per cent in 1980 and over 7 per cent in 1981.

Despite the widely-expressed concern over inflation and economic policies focused on the reduction of inflation, inflation close to a double figure rate has remained. In this study we examine in depth one part of the inflationary process, namely changes in the price of goods. This is undertaken in part to seek answers to the question of why inflation has persisted. But before we come to the detailed discussion of price changes,

1

we need to set out the general context within which prices and their formation are discussed.

The discussion of the causes of inflation and its consequences in developed capitalist economies cannot meaningfully be isolated from the discussion of other aspects of such economies. Views on the operation of such economies must inform discussion on inflation. It may often appear that most discussion by macroeconomists, whether of the monetarist or Keynesian persuasion, does proceed in virtual isolation from a wider consideration of the operation of the economy. This often leads to a consideration of the cost of inflation without much consideration of causes and a stress on a simplistic link between the rate of increase in the money supply and the rate of price inflation. But, the implicit assumptions in most macroeconomics include that of perfectly competitive product markets and labour markets. Out of that assumption comes the view that price changes depend on the level of excess demand (which is the Walrasian adjustment mechanism) and the expected price changes. In the labour market, this is summarised in the expectations-augmented Phillips' curve, that wage changes are related to unemployment (used as a negative proxy for excess demand for labour) and expected price changes.

The general background against which we discuss inflation has two major features. First, an oligopolistic structure is assumed. By this we mean that in most industries a few firms dominate price decisions, and that many wage bargains are struck between employers (and their organisations) and trade unions. Second, money is largely "credit money", that is money which is an asset for the holder but a liability for the bank or other financial institution. Here money "comes into existence along with debts" (Keynes, 1930). In this chapter we explore some of the consequences of these two features.

The distinction between the theory of perfect competition and the associated excess demand theory of price change and the theories of price formation (based on theories of oligopoly, monopoly, etc.) is a theme which runs through the book. In the next chapter, we explore the differences between the two approaches in many dimensions before narrowing down to consider the implications and differences for inflation and price change.

One of the central purposes of this book is to report on empirical investigations into the proximate determinants of price changes in 40 British manufacturing industries over the period 1963 to 1975. These empirical results are summarised and discussed in Chapters 3 and 4. In those chapters we also discuss the results of other investigations into the determinants of price changes. The nature of the theories of price change is surveyed in Chapter 2. From that survey we can indicate how the theories can be subject to empirical validation and the problems involved. However, these theories of price change and the associated theories of price determination have to be placed in context and that is the main purpose of this chapter. We can also indicate how the evidence reported later can be used to throw some light on the Keynesian–monetarist and other debates within macroeconomics.

DEBATES WITHIN MACROECONOMICS

The resurgence of the neo-classical pre-Keynesian macroeconomics in the guise of monetarism can be linked in part with the increased rates of inflation in capitalist economies from the mid-1960s onwards. It is clear, without implying anything about the direction of causation, that any significant inflation will be associated with continuing increases in the money supply. Thus it is almost inevitable that a period of inflation would renew interest in money and monetary policy after the period of relative neglect by the then prevailing Keynesian orthodoxy. But the monetarist counter-revolution has involved much more than merely stressing monetary policy rather than fiscal policy.[1] Much emphasis has been placed within the monetarist approach on the stability of the private sector of the economy, and that stability rests heavily on price flexibility (Modigliani, 1977). The Keynesian explanation of unemployment rests at some point on a failure of prices and wages to change relative to each other and relative to the money supply so as to restore full employment. When the necessary adjustment involved a fall in wages and/or prices, the argument was used that as a practical matter reductions in wages and prices were slow to occur. But in the context of generally rising prices, changes in relative prices can often take place without reductions in absolute prices. Thus inflationary experience weakened the rationale for the price rigidity required by the Keynesian analysis to explain unemployment.[2]

Friedman (1970) argued that the difference between Keynesian and monetarists could be summarised within the IS–LM framework (implicitly seen as accepted by both schools of thought) by saying that Keynesians assumed a fixed price level, whilst monetarists assumed a fixed level of output. Under a Keynesian regime, the economy was seen as adjusting to external shocks by output and employment changes, whilst prices remain unaffected (specifically by changes in the level of output). Under a monetarist regime, the response to external shocks would be prices changing in order that full employment would be restored, thereby determining the level of output. It would perhaps be better to pose the question as to whether the price level is to be regarded as exogenously determined (relative to the economic factors included in the model) or whether the price level does respond to economic factors such as the level of demand.

The literature on the reappraisal of Keynesian economics (e.g. Clower, 1965; Barro and Grossman, 1976) has stressed the notion that following changes in the composition of demand, prices and wages were slow to adjust, whilst the monetarists assumption has usually been that prices and wages adjust rapidly and full employment quickly restored. It is not only a question of the speed of adjustment. For when prices do not adjust instantaneously to clear markets, then consideration must be given to what happens in disequilibrium. In Figure 1.1, demand and supply curves are drawn for a market. When the price is as p_1, then supply exceeds demand, and it is usually assumed that the quantity actually traded in these circumstances would be dictated by demand, i.e. at Q_1. Then the suppliers are not able to sell the amount anticipated (which at price p_1 would be Q_2), and their actual revenue ($p_1 Q_1$) would be less than anticipated ($p_1 Q_2$). If this were a product market, then the firms faced with lower than anticipated revenue may respond by reducing production in subsequent periods, and in doing so reduce their demand for inputs from other firms and for labour. If this were a labour market, then household income is lower than anticipated, and consumer expenditure could be expected to fall. In either event, there would be a deflationary bias introduced into the economy. The disequilibrium situation could have arisen from many reasons, including sudden shifts in the composition of demand. But the deflationary bias in markets where price is above equilibrium is not compensated by reflationary biases in other markets where the price is below equilibrium. The deflationary process which follows from disequilibrium may be absorbed by stocks. For example, a shortfall in household income may not lead to a fall in consumer expenditure if there are stocks of money and other wealth held by the households which they can use to finance expenditure.

CONFLICT AND INFLATION

Much of the above debate takes for granted that markets are perfectly competitive with talk of demand and supply curves and functions and

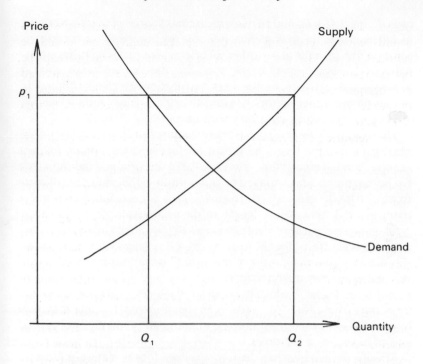

FIGURE 1.1 *Demand and supply curves*

the assumption that economic agents are price-takers. We discuss some of the problems with a perfectly competitive approach in the next chapter in theoretical terms and in Chapter Three in empirical terms. In Chapter Two, we argue that most theories of price determination (and hence of price change) depart from this competitive view, and regard firms as price-makers. Further, firms can be viewed as fixing price as a mark-up over costs, where the determinants of the mark-up depend on which theory is used. Indeed, it can be argued that almost all studies at the micro-level on pricing have focused on questions such as whether the mark-up is constant or not (with respect to demand), on which costs are taken into consideration, etc. and take for granted that firms do not operate, in any meaningful sense, in a perfectly competitive market. Exceptions to this would be studies concerned with the primary commodity and financial markets. But for industrial prices and the like, mark-up pricing of some description is usually presumed. In terms of macro-economics, the presumption of mark-up pricing rather than prices set in competitive markets is a significant change. Before considering that, it should be made clear that theories of mark-up pricing include not only theories such as full-cost pricing where the mark-up is constant, but also the many other theories where price can be interpreted as a mark-up over costs. For the present we write this as $p = m(q, Z).C(q)$ where m is the mark-up function, which may depend on output (q) and other factors (Z) and C is the average costs which are marked up and which may vary with output.

This approach to pricing has many features of importance, and we highlight a number here (and return for further discussion in the next chapter). First, it is clear that prices are based on costs, and indicates that the pricing procedure envisaged operates through the estimation of costs to which a mark-up is applied. The mark-up is not necessarily constant, a point which is discussed at length in the next chapter.

Secondly, the mark-up yields an excess of price over average costs, and a surplus is generated for the firm. An important element covered by the surplus is the reported profits of the firm. Thus, at least in the short run, this indicates that an important ingredient in the determination of profits is the degree to which firms are able and desire to achieve a mark-up of price over costs. This leads to, in the short-run, the determination of profits is unhitched from notions of marginal productivity of capital and of recompense for thrift.

Thirdly, the mark-up has clear implications for the real wage. Writing total (marked-up) costs as $w . L + f . F$, where w is wage, L is labour inputs, f price index of non-labour inputs and F their volume, the price equation given above can be re-written to give:

$$w/p = (Q/mL) - (fF/pL)$$

Thus, the real wage is strongly conditioned by the mark-up (m), labour productivity (Q/L) and the cost of non-labour inputs (f/p).

Fourthly, the volume of profits is dependent on both the mark-up and the level of output, with the latter dependent on the level of demand in the economy. In turn, the level of demand is likely to be strongly influenced by expenditure on investment. Attempts to raise the volume of profits (by, for example, raising the mark-up) would be counter-productive unless expenditure on investment rises to maintain the level of demand. Thus, the realisation of profits requires that expenditure on investment is at an appropriate level.

Fifthly, the effect of demand on prices is seen as likely to be small. Firms are pictured as facing a level of nominal demand, which they divide up into price and output, depending on their costs and their objectives. A rise in demand would be expected normally to lead to a rise in output and in price. Price would be constant with respect to output if the mark-up function and average costs were constant with respect to output. It is often assumed that the determinants of the mark-up (e.g. the elasticity of demand) and average costs are relatively insensitive to output changes. This would lead to the belief that a change in the level of demand would mainly filter through into output changes rather than price changes (for a more formal analysis see pp. 22–36 below).

It can be seen from above that the price mark-up mechanism has implications for the real wage and for profits. The latter are not fully determined by the mark-up price mechanism for, *inter alia*, the level of output has to be determined. The level of output prices, and thereby the real wage and profits, depend on the cost of imported inputs. A full consideration would also need to bring government activity into the picture, particularly in terms of taxation.

Four broad groups can be identified in this type of approach – workers striving for real wages, firms for profits, and the foreign sector for revenue from imported inputs and the government for tax revenue. There will be a conflict between these four groups for sharing out real income. There will also be important conflicts within each of the groups, but here we focus on the inter-group conflicts. Each group makes claims on national income, and there is no strong reason why the claim should always be compatible. But the "reconciliation" of the claims of these four major groupings can come through many routes. The claims of the foreign sector may be varied through changes in the exchange rate, import substitution etc. Workers and owners of firms may offset attempts to increase taxation by trying effectively to shift the taxation on to others. Two particular routes for "reconciliation" are of significance here. The first is that efforts are made by groups to persuade others that their claims are too high. The clearest examples of this in the British context has been the use of income policies and other exhortation by governments to persuade or compel workers to accept lower wages. The second route is through changes in the level of demand. Broadly speaking, we have seen above that the volume of profits depends on output, and also that the mark-up can also depend on output. If that is the case, then the volume and share of profits in revenue varies with the level of output and of demand. So far as workers are concerned, their demands for real wages may be modified by the level of unemployment, which in turn depends on the level of output and demand. Thus the level of output could be seen as establishing a "reconciliation" between the claims for profits and those for real wages. Models in this spirit are presented in Rowthorn (1977) and Sawyer (1982a), (1982b).

Inflation is then seen as arising from, in the first instance, attempts by one or more groups to increase their share of income. One group's income rise is another group's cost rise (and real income decrease). The groups suffering the cost rise are likely to respond by seeking to raise their own prices (whether product price, wages, taxation, etc.) and thereby restore their own income (in real terms), raise costs for others. The continuation of inflation once it has become established may arise from the expectation of future inflation. But we would stress that each economic agent is a small cog in a large wheel, and suffers from cost rises which appear to that agent to necessitate price increases. For example, for an individual firm profits are relatively small proportion of sales revenue (of the order of 20 per cent) and hence a rise in costs which was not offset by a price rise would have a disproportionate effect on profits. Suppose that costs account for 80 per cent of sales revenue, and rise by 10 per cent; if the price of output remains unchanged profits would fall by 40 per cent, whilst a 5 per cent rise in price would still leave profits down by 15 per cent in money terms and down 20 per cent in terms of the proportion of sales revenue. Thus at the level of the firm the experience of inflation is seen as rises in costs which need to be passed on as price rises if profits are to be protected. This focuses on the *experience* of, rather than the *expectation* of, inflation as a reason for the persistent of inflation. We could add, though, that the expectation of future inflation may encourage firms to raise their prices in response to cost increases in that they would then believe that since other firms' prices are rising the demand for their own output would be less effected than otherwise. Similar types of argument would apply to workers.

The triggering of an upsurge in inflation can arise from many directions. In the British context, attention has often been paid by attempts by the government to increase their share of taxation (e.g. in the late 1960s), and by the foreign sector (e.g. the OPEC oilprice rise). The imposition of higher taxation and import prices leads to a fall in post-tax real wages which can trigger off attempts to restore their value by higher money wages. The higher money wages, as well as higher imported input prices and taxation, would lead to higher prices as firms attempt to defend their profit margins.

This essentially conflict theory of inflation focuses on the struggle over income shares between workers, firms, government and the foreign sector. But the continuation of inflation relies on the notion that each economic agent will strive to pass on cost increases as price increases in order to maintain the real value of their income. The continuation of inflation will generally also require the continued expansion of the money supply. Some price rises may be absorbed without a corresponding rise in the money supply, and hence the velocity of circulation rises. But continued inflation without a corresponding rise in the money supply would require continued rises in the velocity of circulation, and this we take to be unlikely.

However, we view the money supply as largely endogenous and developing in response to the demand for money. There are two important features of the money supply relevant here. First, money is largely credit money (that is money which is a credit balance with a bank). This means that whilst money is an asset so far as the holder of the credit balance is concerned, it is a liability so far as the bank is concerned. Further, the creation of money occurs alongside the creation of loans and debts. For example, a loan made by a bank creates a favourable balance in the bank account of the individual borrower (which is passed on to others as it is spent). The borrower has the favourable bank balance (which is an asset to the borrower) offset by the debt to the bank. Thus "money does not enter the system like manna from heaven – or from the sky via Milton Friedman's helicopter. Nor is it simply the creature of the central bank's policies" (Moore, 1979).

The second feature of money is that its precise definition is difficult to make, and the boundaries of the money supply respond to the demands for money. Thus attempts by government to control one definition of the money supply (e.g. sterling M3) at a level below the demands made for that definition would be anticipated to lead to the expansion of the close substitutes for that particular definition of money.

The endogenous nature of credit money and the fact that production takes time and needs to be financed interact in our explanation of one part of the inflationary process. When a firm increases expenditure on inputs, then that increased expenditure must be financed. The increased expenditure may arise from a desire to expand output which requires an increased volume of inputs or from the requirements of paying higher prices for the inputs. In either case, the firm has to increase borrowing from banks or to run down their liquid assets to finance the increased expenditure. The use of the increased borrowing option would lead to increases in the money supply. In both cases if the firm reaps higher revenue (whether from increased output or higher prices) then they will be able to continue to finance higher expenditure in the future. The increase in the money supply, in response to higher input prices, is a necessary feature of inflation (except in cases where there is "excess" liquid assets, when effectively increased velocity of circulation can accommodate the increased prices) in permitting firms to make increased payments for inputs, which leads in turn to increased price for output.

Thus at the level of the firm, an increase in input prices leads to an increased requirement for money (to finance the purchase of inputs) and to an increased supply of money. If the increased supply of money were not forthcoming then some combination of reduced purchase of inputs and of lower (than otherwise) increases in input prices is required.

This view also indicates that once inflation is established within the economy, it becomes difficult to dislodge. For, to state the obvious, the slowing down of price and wage increases for a particular firm or group of workers will require that at the time of implementation the profits of that firm or the real wages of the workers will decline. This arises from the retrospective, rather than prospective, nature of the approach outlined here. This stands in contrast with the more conventional monetarist approach which often suggests that the costs associated with lowering the rate of inflation are the "costs" of revising downwards inflationary expectations and the loss of output and employment which are associated with those downward revisions. In our approach the costs are larger because there is redistribution of income as well as the loss of output involved in forcing the rate of inflation downwards. The loss of output is seen as greater in that changes in demand are seen as having little impact on wage and price change. It is *changes* in demand, not *lower* demand, which reduces inflation.

COSTS OF INFLATION

The conventional approach to inflation has tended to stress the distinction between anticipated and unanticipated inflation. It is argued that anticipated inflation does not in the main affect real outcomes (in terms of output, employment, relative prices), since that inflation has been anticipated and incorporated into the decision-making process. Unanticipated inflation is seen as having real effects (where, for example, it is often argued that price inflation above that anticipated stimulates output),[3] creating difficulties for decision-making and redistributing income in an "arbitrary" fashion. The costs of anticipated inflation are then seen as arising from changes in the demand for money. The argument is basically that the demand for money (in real terms) depends (negatively) on the nominal rate of interest. For whilst money yields a zero rate of interest other financial assets yield a positive nominal rate of interest. Rises in the (anticipated) rate of inflation raises nominal interest rates and reduces the demand for money (in real terms). This reduction in the demand for money, it is argued, imposes costs on the economy. This can be seen in terms of the loss of consumer surplus resulting from a rise in nominal interest rates.[4] These costs are sometimes summarised as "shoe-leather" costs. The lower demand for money holdings implies that individuals hold lower balances of money from which expenditure is financed, but higher balances of other financial assets which are turned into money when the corresponding purchasing power is required. With a lower average balance of money, there are more occasions on which funds are switched from non-money financial assets into money, thereby incurring the higher costs associated with these transactions (such as the shoe-leather and time costs from visiting a bank or other financial institution to give instructions to switch funds).[5] Given the apparent wide-spread concern about inflation, these costs appear rather trivial. In response to this argument, Tobin (1972) indicated that "I suspect that intelligent laymen would be utterly astounded if they realized that *this* is the great evil economists are talking about. They have imagined a much more devastating cataclysm, with Vesuvius vengefully punishing the sinners below. Extra trips between savings banks and commercial banks? What an anti-climax!"

Concern over inflation becomes more understandable if a conflict approach is adopted. The intensification of inflation arises from the intensification of conflict, whereby one or more groups seek to increase their share of national income and others seek to defend their share. For the groups seeking to increase their share, there is the frustration arising from seeing some of the initial gains from a price or wage rise being dissipated as other groups respond. For those other groups, there is the anger of seeing their share diminished and the costs of restoring (if only partially) their share.[6]

CONCLUSIONS

In the next three chapters we will examine empirically and theoretically various approaches to price formation, emphasising the difference between price-taking behaviour under competitive conditions and price making behaviour under oligopolistic conditions. Our empirical work will also seek to discover whether demand changes have any influence on price changes. In the concluding chapter, we will link the discussion in this chapter with the empirical results.

2 Theories of Pricing

INTRODUCTION

An important part of the inflationary process is the determination of prices and price change behaviour. It is not, of course, the whole story for consideration has to be given to other important features such as the determination of the money supply, of wages and of the exchange rate. In the previous chapter we sketched the background and now turn to a detailed consideration of price behaviour.

Theories of price determination are closely linked to theories of the firm, and indeed the prediction of price and output changes following specified changes has often been seen as the major role of theories of the firm (Machlup, 1967). A basic distinction amongst theories of the firm can be made between theories in which firms are essentially price-takers and those theories in which firms are price-makers. In practice the first group consists only of the theory of perfect competition but, as will be seen below, there are many interpretations of perfect competition in terms of price change determination. In contrast, the second group of theories contains a large number of theories, including monopoly, oligopoly (a category which contains several theories), full-cost pricing, etc. and the more important of these are discussed below in respect of price determination.[1]

The theory of perfect competition combines the attributes of free entry into the industry and an homogeneous product. The second attribute means that an individual firm has no discretion over the price to charge (at least if the firm wishes to retain any custom), whilst the free entry condition removes discretion from the existing firms as a group.[2] In contrast, price-making theories provide discretion over price for firms, arising from blockaded entry into the industry and/or differentiated products. This discretion allows the possibility of firms being able to pursue a variety of objectives. In price-making theories prices are *administered* in the sense that the firm is (or can be) pictured as determining prices in pursuit of its objectives, and then declaring those prices as ones at which it is prepared to trade. Potential customers are faced in the short-term with a take-or-leave-it situation. In making their decisions, firms are assumed to make estimates of how customers will react to various prices in terms of quantity demanded. In other words, firms are pictured as dealing with an anonymous market in which a firm puts up a sign indicating the price of its output and customers buy or not buy as they choose.

In reality, the picture is much more complex in two ways which concern us here. First, many transactions are not between firms and final consumers, but between firms and firms. This means that the demand curve facing a firm is not directly based on household preferences but on the attitudes and assumptions of other firms. It is also likely that the number of potential customers for a firm is, in some relevant sense, small. Hence, instead of a situation in which a firm faces a large number of households as potential customers, there may often be situations where a firm faces a relatively small number of firms. In this latter case, the market situation may be approaching bilateral oligopoly (where there are few buyers and few sellers).

Secondly, firms as sellers and firms as buyers are likely to deal with each other on a continuing face-to-face basis. This opens up the way for deals to be struck between buyer and seller and moves away from the picture of the seller setting a price on a take-it-or-leave it basis. These two complexities combine to lead to a picture in which price is determined by the interaction of buyers and sellers, but not in a way pictured by demand-and-supply models but through bargaining etc. (Andrews, 1949, 1964).

The distinction between price-taking theories and price-making ones is, however, much sharper and more important than would be indicated by the preceding discussion. For quite a different view of profits and the determinants of income distribution is also involved. Under conditions of perfect competition each factor will, in equilibrium, be paid the equivalent of its marginal product.[3] The marginal productivity theory is not without its problems, but here we wish to focus on the nature of the profits and the determination of income distribution.[4] First, factors are not distinctive from each others. There is no particular distinction made between, say, labour, material inputs and capital equipment. Each is paid the equivalent of its marginal product. Second, the firm is not specifically a capitalist one in the sense that if there is a residual from revenue after factors have been paid their marginal product, there is nothing in the theory which would indicate to whom that residual would be paid. In particular, there is no requirement within the theory that the owners of capital receive it. Further, in equilibrium, there is no residual to be paid out. Third, the marginal productivity theory provides a theory of the demand for factors, which needs to be placed alongside the supply of factors for the price of each factor to be determined. Fourth, profits (in the sense of the return to the owners of capital) are determined by the interplay of the demand for and supply of "capital." The demand for capital is linked to the marginal productivity of capital equipment, which reflects the additional output which can be attributed to the use of more capital equipment. In turn, the use of more capital equipment permits a more "round-about" method of production. The supply of finance (for capital equipment) is linked with abstinence from consumption, and the rate of interest on finance is seen as a reward for abstinence. The demand for capital equipment and the supply of finance capital are then brought together to determine the rate of interest and capital in use.

A number of writers, including Dobb (1973), Harris (1978), Howard (1983), Meek (1977), have pointed to the existence of two broad streams of thought in economic theory which have been important during the past two centuries. The dominant approach during the past century and the current orthodoxy is, of course, the neo-classical approach. "In general, the central feature of neo-classical analysis is that the problem of distribution, conceived in terms of a society of atomistic individuals, is solved entirely within the sphere of exchange as related to exchange of factor services and the exchange of products. Underlying this analysis is the conception of a society *without* classes . . .". (Harris, 1978, p. 19). In equilibrium, the price of a good is such that the revenue gained from that good is equal to the sum of factor payments where each factor is paid the equivalent of its marginal physical product.

The other stream, variously labelled the classical tradition, the Ricardian-Marxian approach, has a number of characteristics of interest for our current discussion. These characteristics include the idea that "income distribution is treated as being the result of social insitutions (e.g. property ownership) and social relations" (Dobb, 1973, p. 34), and that "the economic process (is conceived) as involving the creation of a *surplus*, over and above the needs of input replacement and workers' consumption, that was appropriated as profit, interest and rent". (Steadman, 1981). Further "there is a kind of principle which explains price in terms of man's activities and relations *as a producer*" (Meek, 1977, p. 153), and an asymmetry between labour and other inputs (Steadman, 1981).

We argue that the theories of pricing considered below, other than that of perfect competition, can be seen as closer to the classical than to the neo-classical tradition. There is not an exact fit between the theories of pricing and the classical tradition, and there are many aspects of the classical tradition which are not touched by the theories of pricing. However, the theories of pricing share some of the characteristics of classical economics listed above. The social institutions involved are capitalist firms involved in production for profit (whether as an objective in itself or a means to other ends). As will be indicated below, the price can be viewed as a mark-up over certain payments (usually labelled as costs) which result in the profits being seen as part of the surplus of revenue over the marked-up costs. Whilst production is not stressed, the focus is on the price determination by producers, and the emphasis is on producers rather than consumers, on supply conditions rather than demand conditions. The theories considered are only intended to apply to the prices of goods and services, and not to the price of labour (i.e. wages). Wages would be considered as determined by quite different forces, e.g. through the process of collective bargaining.

A major task of the discussion below is to indicate how each theory of price-making generates a mark-up view of pricing, and what each theory says about the determinant of the mark-up. In the last chapter, we wrote price as a mark-up over costs in the form $p = m(q, Z).C(q)$. A rearrangement of that equation allows the calculation of a surplus (of revenue over marked-up costs) of $S = (p - C).q = (m(q, Z) - 1).C(q).q$. The surplus may cover not only reported profits but also provide for other payments such as top managerial incomes, and to allow for this we write $S = \pi + F$, where π is reported profits and F other payments out of the surplus. Then it is simple to write.

$$\pi = (m(q, Z) - 1).C(q).q - F.$$

Here we have space only to highlight a few features of this equation. First, profits are seen as closely linked to the notion of a surplus (of revenue over costs). Thus profits are linked to the ability and desire of firms to achieve a mark-up of price over costs and thereby extract a surplus.

Second, price-making theories have to be set within a specific economic environment, which indicates which payments are regarded as costs to the firm and which are regarded as income to the controllers of the firm. For example, a labour-managed firm would treat payments for finance capital as a cost and the income of its worker-members would come out of the surplus (of revenue over costs). The economic environment in the analysis below will be taken to be a capitalist one, in the sense that the shareholders are the owners of the firm and the claimants of any residual. Some of the theories are further restricted in application. For example, the sales maximisation theory of Baumol (1959) is only intended to apply to managerial-controlled firms. Thus, in contrast to the theory of perfect competition, the price-making theories are not generally intended to be universally applicable.

Third, there are two types of costs so far as the firm is concerned – those which are marked-up (and included in the C-function) and those which are not marked-up (and included in F above). The costs which are marked-up help to generate a surplus so far as the firm is concerned. A rise in those costs would lead to a rise in the surplus S, provided that the mark-up and the level of demand were maintained. Profits would rise by more than the rise in the surplus, if the costs included in F do not rise. The costs which are not marked-up do not help to generate a surplus, and increases in such costs detract from profits in a one-for-one manner.

Although not directly relevant to our discussion on changes in the price output, we can note that the competitive approach tends to stress the similarities in the forces determining price and wage changes. In particular, excess demand is seen as a major common factor, with the excess demand for labour seen as leading to changes in the price of labour (i.e. wages) whereas excess demand for output leads to changes in the price of output. But in an oligopolistic approach, the forces determining prices of output and those determining wages are, at one level, different. For output prices are seen as determined by the objectives of firms, their drive for profits and their ability to obtain profits, whilst wages are seen as determined through collective bargaining and the forces which influence the outcome of that bargaining. At another level, the forces at work are seen as similar in that the determination of prices and wages are the outcome of conflict over the distribution of income.

The distinction between prices determined in competitive markets and those determined in oligopolistic ones is similar to the distinction which Kalecki (1971) made between "demand-determined" and "cost-determined" prices. He argued that "short-term price changes may be classified into two broad groups; those determined mainly by changes in cost of production and those determined mainly by changes in demand. Generally speaking, changes in the prices of finished goods are 'cost-determined'; while changes in the prices of raw materials inclusive of primary foodstuffs are 'demand determined'. The prices of finished goods are affected, of course, by any 'demand-determined' changes in the prices of raw materials but it is through the channel of *costs* that this influence is transmitted. It is clear that these two types of price formation arise out of different conditions of supply". In the next sections we will explore these distinctions in detail. Our main divergence from Kalecki is that we stress the role of the level of *excess* demand rather than changes in demand in the competitive market approach. We also allow within the "cost-determined" prices for some influence of demand changes, and a main focus of our empirical investigations is whether in practice demand influences are significant.

Our discussion begins with a consideration of price-taking theory (of perfect competition), from which we derive some equations linking price changes to excess demand and expected price and cost changes. These equations are then estimated in the next chapter. The longer part of our discussion involves price-making theories. In this discussion, we seek to establish that there is a price change equation which can be regarded as common to all these theories, which forms the basis of our estimation in Chapter 4.

PRICE-TAKING THEORIES[5]

The basis of the theory of perfect competition is that each firm faces a price, which is unaffected by its own actions, and adjusts output such that marginal cost is equated with price to ensure (short-run) profit maximisation. Equilibrium for the industry is achieved when there are no abnormal profits which requires that $p = $ m.c. $= $ a.c. (where m.c. is marginal costs, a.c. average costs) with average costs including the "normal" payments to capital. The theory of perfect competition relates to price levels and not to price changes. It is usually assumed that a Walrasian adjustment mechanism operates whereby price changes depend on the level of excess demand. In an inflationary context, we interpret price changes to mean the proportionate rate of change of prices, which we signify by $\dot{p}$ and throughout a dot over a variable will be used to signify proportionate rate of change of the variable, i.e. $\dot{x} = (1/x)(dx/dt)$. Using X to signify excess demand for output, the Walrasian adjustment mechanism can be written as $\dot{p} = f(X)$.

The basic dilemma involved with price-taking approach is that if all economic agents are price-takers, how do prices ever change? (Arrow 1959). Thus some element of price-making has to be introduced to explain price changes, whilst retaining the essential spirit of competitive price behaviour. Early writing in this area postulated the existence of an external agent whose function was that of price-making. Thus Walras (Walras, 1954) in his discussion of general equilibrium postulated an auctioneer who declared a set of prices, collected demands and offers at those prices, and then adjusted prices raising those where demand exceeded supply and lowering those where supply exceeded demand. Eventually a set of prices would be reached at which demands and offers would be in equilibrium. But only when that set of equilibrium prices had been reached was actual trading permitted, and the theory ruled out trading at disequilibrium prices. The problems which arise in the absence of an auctioneer have been much discussed within the context of the reappraisal of Keynesian economics. In the view of Leijonhufvud (1967), "the only thing which Keynes 'removed' from the foundations of classical theory was the *deus ex machina* – the auctioneer which is assumed to furnish, without charge, all the information needed to obtain the perfect co-ordination of the activities of all traders in the present and through the future".

Our immediate concern is with the theories of price adjustment which are based on competitive conditions. These theories are intended to apply to well-defined product markets (cf. pp. 41–3 below). In our discussion here when we talk of output and price, we mean the output of a particular product, and price is the price of that product. We begin with the Walrasian adjustment mechanism, viz; $\dot{p} = f(X)$. In the next chapter, this will be one of the equations which are estimated and we discuss there the problems of measuring excess demand. We can treat this as an "as if" theory, in the sense that we test to see whether prices change *as if* they are determined by excess demand, without being able to provide an *explanation* of how excess demand determines price changes.

The second price adjustment equation, widely used in macro-economic models, is $\dot{p} = f((y - \bar{y})/\bar{y}) + \dot{p}^e$ where y is level of output, $\bar{y}$ a normal level or capacity output and $\dot{p}^e$ is the expected rate of change of price and f' is positive. The term $(y - \bar{y})/\bar{y}$ is intended as a proxy for the excess demand for output, and the difficulties of using such a proxy are discussed in the next chapter. It is hard to find an impressive justification for this equation. Laidler (1973), for example, merely states that "the price formation hypothesised . . . is a version of the expectations-augmented Phillips' Curve, applied directly to the determination of a rate of price inflation, however, rather than to the determination of the rate of wage inflation from which the rate of price inflation might be derived by way of some mark-up-adjusted-for productivity change mechanism".

One line of argument which could be used to justify this type of price equation would be based on a market with an element of product differentiation in the form of locational differences in the point-of-sale of otherwise identical products. A firm could seek when setting its price to maintain its relative position in the market in terms of price and market share by raising its prices in line with other prices. Since it has to forecast other prices, it raises its own price in accordance with what it expects other firms to raise their prices by – hence the $\dot{p}^e$ term. When the firm is faced with positive excess demand it may take the opportunity of hoisting price by more than otherwise, and conversely when faced with excess supply it feels the need to protect its position by a slower than otherwise price rise. In this way, the excess demand term would enter the equation given above. A problem with this approach apart from the divergence from the full rigours of perfect competition, is that each firm might realise that other firms would be changing their prices in response to excess demand or supply, and hence calculations of expected price change would take excess demand into account, leaving the excess demand term redundant. Further, there is no allowance for firms to recoup the consequences of past experiences (i.e. the use of expectations which turned out to be incorrect).

The third variant tries to explain price changes in terms of excess demand and expected price and cost changes and was provided by Parkin (1975) (and used in the context of wage inflation by Parkin Sumner and Ward, 1976). Excess demand is demand minus supply, with demand taken as a function of price of the good relative to other prices (p_i/p) and supply as a function of costs relative to price of good (c_i/p_i). Taking a logarithmic form of these functions lead to:

$$X_{it} = a \log c_{it} + b \log p_t - (a+b) \log p_{it} \tag{1}$$

where X_{it} is excess demand for good i in period t.

Firms are postulated to seek to eliminate excess demand within a period,[6] so that:

$$\Delta X_{it} = -X_{it}, \quad \text{i.e.} \quad X_{it} - X_{it-1} = -X_{it-1} \tag{2}$$

From (1) the following equation can be derived:

$$\Delta X_{it} = a\dot{c}_{it} + b\dot{p}_t + (a+b)\dot{p}_{it} \tag{3}$$

where $\dot{c}_{it}$ etc. represents the discrete approximation $\log c_{it} - \log c_{it-1}$ for the proportionate rate of change in c_i etc.[7] Combining (2) and (3) and rearranging leads to:

$$\dot{p}_{it} = (a/a+b)\dot{c}_{it} + (b/a+b)\dot{p}_t + (1/a+b)X_{it-1} \tag{4}$$

where it can be noted that the sum of coefficients on $\dot{c}_{it}$ and $\dot{p}_t$ is unity. But equation (3) can also be written as

$$\dot{p}_{it} = (a/a+b)\dot{c}_{it} + (b/a+b)\dot{p}_t - (1/a+b)\Delta X_{it} \qquad (5)$$

Equation (5) differs from equation (4) in that (4) is intended to be a casual equation in that excess demand causes price change (in order to eliminate excess demand, given the decision rule of the firms), whereas (5) is a noncasual equation of association between excess demand changes and price changes.[8] Further, equation (4) can be estimated either by substitution X_{it-1} from the equivalent of equation (1) or by using a proxy such as deviation of output from trend for excess demand. In contrast equation (5) can only be estimated with proxy measures of X_{it} not derived from (1) or (3).

A major purpose of this line of analysis is the introduction of expectations into a price change equation involving excess demand. In the first approach above involving the Walrasian adjustment mechanism, expectations were not involved, and the second approach considered introduced them in a rather informal way. In this third approach, it is argued that firms change price based on forecast changes in c_i and p since current information on such changes is not available. From this line of argument, we have a slightly amended version of (4):

$$\dot{p}_{it} = (a/a+b)\dot{c}_{it}^e + (b/a+b)\dot{p}_t^{et} + (1/a+b)X_{it-1}. \qquad (4')$$

It is clear that the derivation of (4') takes place outside of the conventional excess demand mechanism. Firms are postulated to seek to eliminate excess demand within the period, which combines elements of competitive behaviour and of price-making behaviour. Two problems arise here. First, we can contrast (4') with a Walrasian adjustment mechanism i.e.[9]

$$\dot{p}_{it} = f(X_{it-1}) \qquad (6)$$

This forcibly indicates the inconsistency between the approach of Parkin (1975) and a conventional excess demand approach. Second, no reason is given why firms would wish collectively to eliminate excess demand within a period, nor is any indication given of the length of the period. When price is above equilibrium so that there is excess supply, a reduction in price and the elimination of the (negative) excess demand leads to lower price and higher output (assuming output traded is minimum of *ex ante* demand and supply), which may lead to higher or lower revenue (depending on the elasticity of demand) and to higher or lower profits. It can be noted that the partial elimination of excess demand within a period (i.e. replacing (2) by $\Delta X_{it} = -\lambda X_{it-1}$) would lead to equation (4) being amended to

$$\dot{p}_{it} = (a/a+b)\dot{c}_{it} + (b/a+b)\dot{p}_t + (\lambda/a+b)X_{it-1} \qquad (4'')$$

But since the value of $(a+b)$ cannot be identified from the estimated coefficients on $\dot{c}_{it}$ and $\dot{p}_t$, there is no change in the prediction concerning the coefficient of X_{it-1}, namely that it is positive.

This particular approach forcibly indicates the non-Keynesian nature of the excess demand approach to price change. Examination of equation (1) above indicates that excess demand is a function only of relative prices, and that demand does *not* depend on the level of aggregate demand or any related concept. In the next chapter, in our discussion of using deviations of output from trend as a proxy for excess demand, will indicate that the use of such a proxy can only carry through if, *inter alia*, excess demand is not a function of aggregate demand. It is interesting to note that if a Keynesian approach is used and demand is taken as a function of aggregate demand, then equation (1) becomes:

$$X_{it} = a \log c_{it} + b \log p_t - (a+b) \log p_{it} + \mathrm{d}\,AD_t \qquad (1')$$

where AD_t is a measure of aggregate demand in period t. Then proceeding as before we arrive at an amended version of (4), i.e.

$$\dot{p}_{it} = (a/a+b)\dot{c}_{it} + (b/a+b)\dot{p}_t + (1/a+b)X_{it-1} + (d/a+b)\Delta AD_t \qquad (4''')$$

Laidler and Parkin (1975) in their survey of inflation attack the work of Godley and Nordhaus (1972) (on which more below) on the grounds that "Godley and Nordhaus specified the rate of price change as depending on *changes* in excess demand. This is an incorrect specification: it is at odds with the usual theory of price setting and with earlier empirical work which had found the *level* of excess demand to be important." We will argue below that this contention is incorrect within the context of the Godley and Nordhaus approach (and indeed of any price-making approach). But further equation (4''') indicates that within the context of the Parkin approach, changes in aggregate demand will only be omitted if a non-Keynesian view is taken in that only relative prices are thought to influence demand and supply. The measure of demand used by Godley and Nordhaus can be seen correlated with measures of aggregate demand.

The formulation used by Parkin (1975) followed above indicated that unit costs enter the supply, and thereby the excess demand, function. But strictly speaking that is incorrect, and c_{it} should be interpretted as an index of input prices. The marginal cost curve, which underlies the supply curve, is assumed to be upward-sloping with respect to output. Assuming that we can write marginal costs as $c.f(q)$ where c is an index of input prices and q is output with $df/dq > 0$). Then price $p = c.f(q)$ leads to supply of output q as a function of p/c. Thus in the above c should be regarded as an index of input prices.

PRICE-MAKING THEORIES

Our discussion of price-making theories begins with the simplest one-monopoly pricing. Within the discussion of that approach it is possible to bring out many points which apply also to the theories discussed subsequently. After the discussion of monopoly pricing, we will deal quickly with a variety of other pricing theories.

The monopolist is portrayed as seeking to maximise profits over a decision period $\pi = p(q).q - C(q)$ where C is total variable (over the decision period) costs. The profit maximisation condition is:

$$d\pi/dq = p(q) + q.dp/dq - dC/dq = 0 \qquad (7)$$

which leads to:

$$p = (e/e - 1).dC/dq = f.dC/dq \qquad (8)$$

where e is the elasticity of demand $(-(p/q)(dq/dp))$ and $f = e/(e-1)$.

This price equation for a monopolist shares a number of interesting features with those equations derived for other theories. First, the decision process involves the choice of output (equation 7), but since the price and output are linked via the demand equation that implies a choice of price (equation (8)). Since over the short-run we observe that firms set a price and then supply output to meeting the resulting demand (followed by subsequent price and output adjustments), and with our interest in prices and inflation, it seems more appropriate to deal with the price rather than the (implicit) output equation. Thus we focus on equation (8) and its equivalents. A related point is that this and other models are set up as instantaneous production models with no allowance for lags between decision to change output and that change occuring. When production takes time, firms have to plan ahead with price and output for some relevant future period determined on the basis of expected demand and cost conditions. We would anticipate that firms plan and do charge a price, say p^*, which would lead to sales of say, q^*, which on the basis of the expected demand conditions and costs maximise profits. The price is then set at p^*, and the firm actually sells, say q', which will often be different from q^*. If the firm actually produces q^*, then inventory changes absorb the difference between q^* and q'. When there is an element of adjustment possible, then it could be anticipated that output will be moved towards q'. But in setting prices, the firm would have to work on the basis of expected output q^*. Hence, when production takes time, firms may well be observed to base price on the costs of expected output.

Secondly, following from the first point and equations (7) and (8), it is clear that price and output are jointly determined variables. Thus in equation (8), although price is on the left hand side of the equation and quantity of output on the right hand side, it cannot be said that a particular level of output *causes* a particular level of price. Later a similar point will arise in connection with price changes and output changes, which will have implications for the estimation of price change equations.

Thirdly, it is clear that price can be regarded as a mark-up over costs (in this case marginal costs). When a firm has little reason to believe that the factors relevant to that mark-up (in this case the elasticity of demand) have changed, then the mark-up would remain unchanged. Further, since factors such as the elasticity of demand (and under oligopoly theory perceived reactions of rivals) are not known with anything approaching certainty, and it is costly to discover changes in those factors, it is quite conceivable that the mark-up will be fairly stable over time.

Fourthly, there is an implied theory of profits involved. In this case, the ratio of profits to sales is $(p(q).q - C(q))/p(q).q = 1 - (C(q)/q)/(f.dC/dq)$. Thus, in this case, the profits/sales ratio depends on the elasticity of demand (via the f-term), and the technical conditions of production reflected in the relationship of average costs $(C(q)/q)$ to marginal costs (dC/dq). It is often argued that average costs and marginal costs are approximately equal, and when that is so the profit/sales ratio becomes $1/e$.

Fifthly, the relationship between price and average cost may vary during the course of a trade cycle. The elasticity of demand may depend on and hence vary with the general level of demand. The ratio of average costs to marginal costs can vary with the level of output, unless both types of costs are constant in which case the ratio is always unity.

Sixthly, the firm is faced with a particular demand conditions, which were summarised by $p(q)$. But that inverse demand function shifts with changes in the level of demand etc., and faced with a specific demand function, the firm determines how it is split up in terms of price and output, although the price and output are required to satisfy the demand although the price and output are required to satisfy the demand conditions.

Our discussion of price changes is aided by making two refinements to the price equation (8). We first make it explicit that the elasticity of demand (e) and hence the f-term can be functions of the level of demand and other variables. We will assume that the level of output rises with the level of demand in real terms and proxy demand by q, and summarise other factors by the vector $\mathbf{Z}$. Then we can write

$$p = f(q, \mathbf{Z}).dC(q)/dq \tag{9}$$

The second amendment is to divide up cost changes into those which arise from changes in input prices and those which arise from changes in the level of output. In terms of the level of costs we wish to write $C(q)$ as a separable function of input prices and the level of output, i.e. $C(q) = g(v).c(q)$, where g is a function of a vector of input prices, v and c is an index of "real" costs (which may depend on the level of output). This particular formalisation can be derived from cost minimisation behaviour, provided that the production function is homothetic and input prices are constant for the firm (see Shephard, 1970). The homothetic production function assumption, whereby the function is a monotonic transformation of a homogeneous function, allows for variations in the degree of returns to scale. The proportions in which inputs are used by a cost-minimising firm using a homothetic production function depend on the relative prices of the inputs and not on the scale on output. Further, the function g is now homogeneous of degree one, so that the same proportionate increase in all input prices would lead to the same increase in g and hence in C (provided that the level of output is maintained). This characterisation is particularly useful for our discussion below in terms of mathematical convenience and we shall use it for that reason.

There may be severe practical difficulties in separating input price changes from output-related costs changes. In the context of cost minimisation with a homothetic production function and parametric prices, there would be little difficulty. But in practice, the input prices faced by the firm may vary with its level of output. Labour costs provide the main example here. As a firm changes the level of output, the labour input changes partly by variations in the hours worked. When overtime is involved, this leads to a variation in the price of the input (say an hour of work) since overtime hours are paid more than standard hours.

Coutts, Godley and Nordhaus (1978) postulate that price changes depend on changes in normalised costs, where the normalisation is that the unit costs of production are calculated as they would be if the firm were producing at some normal level of output. The major part of their normalisation (see their Chapter 2) was to remove the effect of variations in the hours of work. In terms of our previous discussion, this would be interpretted as meeting the problem of variations in the price of the input depending on its use (and the level of output) by calculating its price at some normal level of use and using that price in the v-vector of input prices. Variations in the price from that normal level would then be allocated to the c-function. Coutts, Godley and Nordhaus hypothesise in effect that either real costs and the factors determining the mark-up do not vary with the level of output, leaving prices moving in line with (normalised) input prices or firms ignore any variations in real costs or factors determining the mark-up.

Our analysis (and implicitly that of Coutts, Godley and Nordhaus) is at the firm level. Thus changes in the macroeconomic climate, particularly those related to the level of aggregate demand, employment etc., may still lead to changes in prices through changes in input prices. For example a rise in the cost of labour, arising from a high aggregate demand for labour would show up at the firm level as an input price change. Writing out equation (9) in full:

$$p = f(q, \mathbf{Z}) . g(v) . c'(q) \qquad (9')$$

where c' is the marginal real cost (i.e. the first derivative of c).

This equation can be regarded as one particular version of the general price equation:

$$p = g(v) . h(q, \mathbf{Z}) \qquad (9'')$$

which will form the basis of discussion below.

Differentiating equation (9') with respect to time, and expressing the results in proportionate rate of change form yields:

$$\dot{p} = \dot{f} + \dot{g} + \dot{c}' \qquad (10)$$

Further expansions of the right hand side yields

$$\dot{p} = e_2 \dot{Z} + e_g . \dot{v} + (e_1 + e_c). \dot{q} \qquad (11)$$

where $e_1 = (q/f)(\partial f / \partial q)$, e_2 is a vector with elements $(Z_i/f).(\partial f / \partial Z_i)$
$e_c = (q/c')(\partial c'/\partial q)$ and e_g is vector with elements $((v_i/g)(\partial g/\partial v_i))$ which sum
to unity (since g is homogeneous of degree 1).

This provides an instantaneous price adjustment model, with the
assumption that there are no adjustment costs arising from changing
price or output. We are seeking an equation which will explain quarter-
to-quarter changes in price. We assume that firms will make price
decisions at least quarterly and that the costs of decision-making are
invariant with respect to the size of price change. Under those circumstances, the cost of price adjustment would become irrelevant to these
price changes. If there are costs involved in changing output, this would
show up in terms of the charge in output decided upon, and so affects the
right hand side of our equation.

It can be seen that the conditions for changes in output to have no
relationship with price changes are that $e_1 = e_c = 0$. The first condition is
that the elasticity of demand is invariant with respect to output and the
second that marginal costs are constant with respect to output. The
notable feature of these conditions is that it is often assumed that they
hold. Under those conditions, we would have essentially pure-cost
inflation (at the firm level).

The interpretation and estimation of equation (11) or similar is
complicated by the feature indicated above that price changes and
output changes are jointly determined. The econometric considerations
are discussed in Chapter 4. Although the sum of coefficients on the
change in input prices terms ($\dot{v}$) is unity, it cannot be immediately
concluded that a 1 per cent rise in costs would lead to a 1 per cent rise in
price, for the rise in price would have an effect on sales and hence on
output. Similarly, the impact of demand changes cannot be quickly
assessed. This can be illustrated by using a constant elasticity of demand
function of the form $p^k . q = K$. A change in the general level of demand
for this product is reflected in a change in K, and we have $k . \dot{p} + \dot{q} = \dot{K}$.
Substitution of this equation into equation (11) yields:

$$\dot{p} = 1 + k(e_1 + e_c) = e_g . \dot{v} + (e_1 + e_c)\dot{K} \qquad (12)$$

The effect of a 1 per cent rise in the general level of demand on price
change would be $(e_1 + e_c)/(1 + k(e_1 + e_c))$, and on output change would

be $1/(1 + k(e_1 + e_c))$. One of the factors which would increase demand for output of the firm in question would be increases in the prices of other products. With the demand function homogeneous of degree zero in prices, this would give $p^k . q = K . p_w^k$, where p_w represents general price level. Then we find that a 1 per cent rise in p_w leads to a rise in p of $k(e_1 + e_c)/(1 + k(e_1 + e_c))$ per cent of $k/(1 + k(e_1 + e_c))$ and in q per cent.

In one sense equation (12) provides a division between demand influences and cost influences on price changes, which could correspond to the conventional division between demand-pull and cost-push inflation. But there are some crucial differences. First, this equation has been derived at the firm level (which is here equivalent to the industry level), and what appears as a cost change at the level of the firm or industry can arise from the operation of demand and other factors elsewhere in the economy influencing the input prices paid by this firm or industry. Second, the demand-pull/cost-push distinction is intended to describe the source of excess demand, which in turn leads to price changes, whereas this distinction clearly arises from price-making behaviour. Third, the demand forces here are *changes* in the *demand* rather than the *level* of *excess demand*. This can be related back to the debate between Laidler and Parkin (1975) and Coutts, Godley and Nordhaus (1978) which was mentioned above (p. 21). The price-making approach gives clear support for Coutts, Godley and Nordhaus view, that the pressure of demand on price changes can be tested by relating demand *changes* to price *changes*.

We now move on to consider a general theory of oligopoly, in which the prices set by one firm are likely to be influenced by how other firms in the industry respond and are expected to respond to price changes. The formal model in this context is as follows. The demand for the product of firm i depends on the price charged by that firm (p_i), the price charged by other firms in the industry (represented by the price index p) and other factors summarised by the variable D. The profits function of firm i is then $\pi_i = q_i(p_i, p, D)p_i - C(q_i)$ and the first-order condition for maximisation of short-run profits is:

$$\frac{\partial \pi}{\partial p_i} = \left(\frac{\partial q_i}{\partial p_i} + \frac{\partial q_i}{\partial p}\frac{\partial p}{\partial p_i}\right)\left(p_i - \frac{\partial C}{\partial q_i}\right) + q_i = 0$$

which can be manipulated to yield

$$p_i = \frac{\partial C}{\partial q_i}(e_i - e_i'\alpha)/(e_i - e_i'\alpha - 1) \tag{13}$$

where $e_i = -(p_i/q_i)(\partial q_i/\partial p_i)$, $e_i' = (p/q_i)(\partial q_i/\partial p)$
and $\alpha = (p_i/p)(\partial p/\partial p_i)$.

This can be summarised by saying that the price of firm i is a mark-up over marginal costs with the mark-up determined by the product elasticity of demand (e_i), the cross-elasticity of demand (e_i') and the degree of interdependence between the firms as reflected in the term α. The term $(e_i - e_i'.\alpha)/(e_i - e_i'.\alpha - 1)$ can be interpreted as a formalisation of the notion of the degree of monopoly advanced by Kalecki (1971), (Cowling (1982)). The degree of monopoly is set in part by predetermined factors such as the general nature of the product produced by the industry and the resulting elasticity of demand. But firms can change the nature of products produced and the perception held about them by the consumers through product innovation, advertising and the like. Thus the elasticities involved here are under the influence, if not the control, of the firms involved. Further, the extent of rivalry between firms, influenced by the political and legal environment, would serve to influence the value of α.

By differentiation it can soon be shown that the mark-up of price over marginal costs, given by $(e_i - e_i'\alpha)/(e_i - e_i'\alpha - 1)$, will rise with e_i and α and fall with e_i'. The higher the level of concentration in an industry the higher the value of α would be expected to be, and hence the higher the mark-up of price over marginal cost. General considerations suggest that as the number of firms in an industry decline, the interdependence between firms becomes more apparent, and co-ordination between firms is easier with fewer firms. Further, if the number of products in the industry is larger than the number of firms, then some co-ordination of price changes is inevitable since one firm decides several prices. It might be further expected that, *ceteris paribus*, the value of e_i falls with rises in concentration, for simply with fewer firms in the industry a price cut by one firm has a smaller market from which to draw custom, leading to a smaller rise in demand. These general considerations would indicate that the mark-up rises with concentration.

A specific example of this general approach corresponds to the kinked demand curve (Sweezy, 1939) where $\alpha = 0$ for price rises and $\alpha = 1$ for price reductions, leading to a reluctance for firms to change prices. Our discussion below on the administered price thesis also draws on this approach in that variations in price relative to marginal cost during the course of the trade cycle can be interpretted in terms of variations in the mark-up given above. It is then possible to see whether variations in the mark-up over the trade-cycle are linked with the level of concentration.

The theory of limit-pricing (Modigliani (1958), Bain (1956), Sylos-Labini (1962)) focuses on the conditions of entry into an industry as the key determinant of the mark-up of price over costs. In Modigliani (1958) economies of scale is the major barrier, whilst Bain discusses absolute cost advantage, product differentiation as well as economies of scale as important entry barriers. Spence (1977) stresses the role of excess capacity in deterring entry. In the limit-pricing theory, firms are seen as concerned with the long-run perspective rather than a short-term one, and view the prevention of entry into the industry as serving their long-term interest. A medium amount of super-normal profits which persist is seen as being preferred to higher profits now which induce entry and lower profits in the future. Under limit-pricing, the price is set such that potential entrants into the industry believe that entry will not be profitable in light of existing price and beliefs about price after entry. In the context of Modigliani (1958), with economies of scale forming the barriers to entry, it is assumed that potential entrants believe that existing firms would maintain their output at its current level after the entry of new firms. The prospect for new firms is that the post-entry price is lower than pre-entry price as new firms add their output to that of existing firms. A residual demand curve can be drawn under these circumstances (as RD is Figure 2.1) which is total industry demand minus current output, and under the behavioural assumptions outlined above, forms the demand curve facing potential entrants. The limit-price is indicated in Figure 2.1 being generated by the level of output by existing firms such that the residual demand curve facing potential entrants is everywhere below their cost curves, thereby making entry appear unprofitable. Modigliani gives an approximate formula for the limit-price, when S is the minimum feasible scale of production, p_c the competitive price and e the elasticity of demand, then the limit-price is $p_c(1 + 1/eS)$.

The competitive price is the one which would just cover average costs, so we write that equation as:

$$p = ac \cdot (1 + 1/eS) \tag{14}$$

assuming that the limit-price is actually charged. It can easily be seen that this price equation is of the general form that price is a mark-up over costs, with the mark-up in this case determined by the elasticity of demand and the minimum feasible scale of operation.

The way in which movements in demand over the trade cycle affect the price in such circumstances is not clear-cut. At one extreme, if any hint of

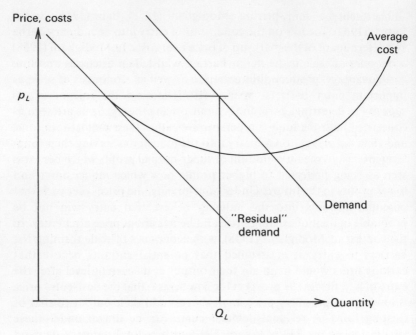

FIGURE 2.1 *Limit-pricing outcome*

post-entry profits induces entry into the industry, then price would have to be maintained in line with the limit-price, and hence (14) applies throughout the trade-cycle. The other extreme would be that entry depended on the prospect of permanent post-entry profits. In which case (14) would provide the average relationship which holds over the course of the business cycle. Under such circumstances firms could, for example, maintain output at a constant level and allow the price to vary (relative to costs) so as to satisfy the demand consideration.

The Modigliani analysis is restrictive in a number of respects. First, it deals with a monopoly situation. With oligopoly situations, the limit-price may provide an upper limit on prices, provided that there is some agreement, tacit or otherwise, that entry should be deterred and the effectiveness of collusion between the firms would determine how close they came to achievement. Further those firms who strive for entry-preventing prices would tend to undercut the prices of other firms. Secondly, each potential entrant is seen as calculating the effect of its own entry, provided that no other entry takes place. But the possibility of multiple entry creates more protection for existing firms as the more entry which occurs the sharper the fall in price falling entry. Third, barriers to entry are limited to economies of scale.

A general view of limit-pricing would indicate that there are various barriers which impede entry into an industry such as economies of scale, advertising and brand loyalty, absolute cost advantages and excess capacity. Some of these could be seen as "states of nature" whilst others are determined by the actions of existing firms. We assume that there is a vector **X** whose elements summarise the height of the various entry barriers. The degree to which firms can mark-up prices above costs depends on a function of **X**, i.e. $p = f(\mathbf{X}) \cdot ac$. This provides a similar but more general outcome to that achieved by the simple limit-pricing theory outlined above.

The remaining theories focus on the internal organisation of the firm, and its impact on the objectives of the firm without paying much regard to the market environment within which it operates.

The first of these is the theory of sales-revenue maximisation introduced by Baumol (1959). In this theory, the firm is viewed as controlled by its managers rather than its shareholders. The managers pursue their own interests, such as income, status, which Baumol argues, are correlated with the size of the firm reflected in sales revenue. Thus managers can be portrayed as seeking to maximise sales revenue. But the shareholders impose a lower limit on the profits which must be earned, which effectively reflects the supply-price of finance capital to the firm. Baumol argues that this profit constraint will be binding on the firm, which means that the firms operates where $\pi = \pi_{min}$, the profit constraint. Hence $p \cdot q - g(v) \cdot c(q) = \pi_{min}$, and then:

$$p = (g(v) \cdot c(q) + \pi_{min})/q \tag{15}$$

For simplicity we suppress reference to advertising in this formulation. The price response of the sales-maximisation firm to changes in other prices would depend in this context on the manner in which the minimum profit constraint evolved. If, for example, shareholders applied the price index of inputs, $g(v)$, then we could write (15) as

$$p = g(v) \cdot (c(q) + A)/q \tag{16}$$

where A is the real value of the minimum profit constraint (measured in a way compatible with the measurement of $c(q)$). If, however, the minimum profit constraint evolved with the price charged by the firm

(15) would become:

$$p = g(v).c(q)/(q - A) \tag{17}$$

If some external price index were judged appropriate then it would not be possible to express (15) in a simple formulation.

During the course of the trade cycle with the level of demand varying if the firms seek to maximise sales revenue in each time interval subject to a profit constraint which is invariant with respect to the level of demand, then equation (15) would hold throughout. An alternative would be that shareholders have higher expectations when demand and output are high so that π_{min} becomes a function of output. If we take this more general case, together with the assumption that the profit constraint evolves with the price index $g(v)$, we can then write (15) as:

$$p = g(v).(c(q) + A(q))/q \tag{18}$$

Thus this leads to a price equation of the general form with price as a mark-up over costs, such that price can be expressed as a multiple of $g(v)$ and a function of output and other factors (which here include the extent of power of shareholders over managers). In this case, if A were constant with respect to output then there would be good reason to think that the mark-up would decline with output since A/q clearly declines as q rises. Thus increases in demand could lead to a fall in the mark-up and thereby to a fall in price.

Some post-Keynesian approaches to pricing have stressed the linkages between prices, profits and investment (e.g. Harcourt and Kenyon, 1976). In our discussion we focus on the model presented by Eichner (Eichner, 1973, 1976). The starting points of his model are two-fold. First, it is assumed that in each oligopolistic industry, the price level and changes in it are determined by the price leader, which is taken to be the least cost producer and whose cost and revenue curves are treated as the marginal portions of the industry supply and demand curves. Secondly, price is related to the need to generate profits, from which investment is financed, and price change is linked with increased demands for investment.

Eichner presents a key price formula as:

$$p = avc + (fc + cl)/(svr.erc) \tag{19}$$

where p is price, avc average variable cost, fc fixed costs, cl the corporate levy, sor standard operating rate and erc engineer-rated capacity.

Average variable costs are conventionally defined, but fixed costs are taken to include managerial salaries, interest and dividend payments but exclude expenditures on research and development and advertising. The reason for this is that the firm (megacorp in Eichner's terminology) is controlled by managerial interests who regard dividends as the cost of satisfying shareholders and expenditure on advertising etc. as enhancing the firm's long-run market position (and hence helping to secure their jobs and salaries). The corporate levy is "the amount of funds available to the megacorp from internal sources to finance investment expenditures" (Eichner, 1976). The denominator of the second-term on the left hand side of (19) indicates that these fixed costs and corporate levy are averaged across standard output when price is calculated. The direction of causation is from a growth target leading to a requirement for investment funds, which leads to the setting of a corporate levy, and thereby to price. It is not necessarily the case that all investment is internally financed. The firm has to take account of the consequences of raising the corporate levy and price, and Eichner sees the main consequences arising from the possibility of substitution effects (or other products for the one in question) and of entry into the industry (with meaningful government intervention seen as a logical but unlikely possibility). The costs of those consequences are then balanced against the costs of raising external finance to determine the corporate levy. We have reported Eichner's views very summarily here to focus on the price decision.

From equation (19) we can see that price depends on three factors, namely average variable costs, fixed costs plus corporate levy, and standard level of output. The average variable costs are assumed constant with respect to output. Thus changes in output do not effect *avc* and, unless the assessment of the standard level of output changes, do not affect the second term of the price equation either. Thus, it could be anticipated that price was constant with respect to short-term fluctuations in output. The longer-term outlook for output and demand have two effects. First, it influences the requirement for investment finance and hence the corporate levy. Thus expectations of future growth influences investment requirements, and thereby the price needed to generate the profits to finance the investment. Secondly, as investment occurs capacity and operating costs change. Eichner (1976) focuses on the role of changes in the demand and supply of additional investment finance leading to price changes. For our purposes, it is more relevant to focus on demand and input price changes. Changes in the price of inputs entering the calculations of average variable costs, fixed costs or the corporate levy will lead to price changes in this model. If, for simplicity, we expressed equation (19) as

$$p = avc + afc = avc(1 + afc/avc) \qquad (19')$$

where *afc* is average fixed costs plus corporate levy calculated at standard level of output. Thus price is a constant mark-up over average variable costs (which are assumed constant with respect to output) provided that prices influencing *avc* and those influencing *afc* move together.

A rather different approach to the firm, based on the work of Simon (1959) and other authors such as Cyert and March (1963), stresses the firm as an organisation. As such there is emphasis on the difficulties of formulating objectives for an organisation, and particularly that this leads to satisfying behaviour. This essentially means that firms continue in a grove provided that the results achieved are judged satisfactory. In the context of pricing, this can be interpretted in terms of the full-cost pricing theory. Under this theory, a firm sets its price with reference to average direct costs, with a fixed mark-up i.e.

$$p = (1 + d).g(v).C^*(q) \qquad (20)$$

where *d* is the mark-up and C^* average direct costs. It is implicit in this theory that the mark-up is generally attainable. The mark-up within the satisficing approach is determined by the organisational requirements of the firm. It can also be interpretted within the context of the preceding theories in the context of large organisations. The senior managements can form a view on the profit margin which should be aimed for in each line of business, based on its assessment of demand, competitors actions, etc. These views on the optimal profit margin can be passed down the line to the product managers, etc. It is also a means by which the overheads of the firm can be allocated in an accounting sense to the various products made by the firm. It is fairly clear from (20) that the full cost-pricing theory fits into the general pattern, and places considerable emphasis on the role of costs in determining prices. Demand, both in respect of the level of aggregate demand and of price of competing products, is seen as having a limited role on price and thereby mainly determines the level of output. This arises since the profit margin is assumed as constant with respect to output and further because it is often assumed within this theory (e.g. Hall and Hitch, 1939) that average direct costs are constant with respect to output.

Andrews (1949) put forward the view that "the price which a business will normally quote for a particular product will equal the estimated average direct costs *plus* a costing margin", and that the "average direct costs will tend to remain at a constant level, whatever, the output that is being produced, given the prices of direct-cost factors of production and ignoring any extraordinary increase in direct costs (due e.g. to overtime wages being paid for extra output in the short period)", and "that given the prices of the direct factors of production, price will tend to remain unchanged, whatever the level of its output".

Godley and Nordhaus (1972) put forward a similar view when they postulate that "output price is set by taking a constant percentage over average normal historical current cost". In some respects this "normal price hypothesis" can be seen to represent the ultimate expression of the view that price depends only on costs. For the idea that "prices are determined by normal (or standard) costs, and that they do not react to temporary, or cyclically reversible, changes in either demand or cost" denies any indirect effect of demand on prices operating via costs as well as denying the direct effect.

These views that price is based on some notion of normalised costs are particularly concerned with the impact of short-run variations in output on price. These variations in output do not run out of a range which the firm could cope with. In particular, the level of output does not approach the physical capacity level, nor drop to such low levels that the surplus of revenue over variables costs does not cover fixed costs. The longer term prospective for demand may influence capacity, but not directly the pricing decision. These views leave the profit margin undetermined, and for that one needs to draw on the various theories discussed immediately above. Further, these authors do not draw on a formal analysis of price determination, but see the price as a mark-up over normal costs as a useful approximation to what firms actually do.

In summary, this section on price-making theories has argued for a general price equation of the form:

$$p = h(q, \mathbf{Z}).g(v) \tag{21}$$

The variable $\mathbf{Z}$ summarises the other factors (besides output) which influences the mark-up. The factors which enter $\mathbf{Z}$ clearly differ as between the theories, and the above discussion has indicated which factors enter $\mathbf{Z}$ in each theory. Since these other factors are often assumed to be slowly changing and/or difficult to measure we arrive at a price change equation which by ignoring changes in $\mathbf{Z}$ is of the form:

$$\dot{p} = e_g.\dot{v} + e_h.\dot{q} \tag{22}$$

where $e_h = (q/h)(\partial h/\partial q)$

Equation (22) is particularly useful in that it enables us to investigate the general price-making theories and the empirical values of e_g and e_h without being committed to a particular variant of that approach. Thus this equation forms the basis of much of our empirical work reported in Chapter 4.

ADMINISTERED PRICE THESIS

Beginning with Means (1936) there has been sporadic controversy over what is usually labelled the administered price thesis. There has been considerable difficulty in pinning down exactly what the administered price thesis is, and on this see Beals (1975), Lustgarten (1975). There are two important strands within the administered price thesis, which can be linked back with our previous discussion. The first strand is that most prices are administered in the sense that the producer sets a price at which it is prepared to trade. Thus, as pointed out above, most prices are administered by a firm usually the producer rather than being set for the firm by an anonymous market. Arising out of this, prices were thought to change less frequently than they did under competitive circumstances. In competitive markets such as those in many primary products, prices were seen to change frequently, often from minute to minute in the commodity markets.

It has been argued that whilst the prices announced by firms (i.e. list prices) may be infrequently changed, partly because of the costs associated with changing price catalogues etc., there may be changes in the prices (i.e. transaction prices) actually charged. When a situation approaching bilateral oligopoly exists, then the list price could be viewed as the opening bid in negotiations between firms over the price. The firm selling may, it is argued, be prepared to trim prices below those listed more during a slump than during a boom. Thus it is argued evidence on the stability of list prices may be a misleading indication of the behaviour of traded prices. But studies such as Coutts, Godley and Nordhaus (1978) have cast doubt on the empirical significance of this argument.

It could also be argued that those industries where products are often produced to the specifications of the customer create problems. Price indices for such industries would be very difficult to construct (and so such industries are often omitted from economic studies) yet profit margins in those industries could well respond to demand. For simply inhibitions through printed price lists etc. are clearly absent in such cases. There is a further complication that in such industries prices may be set in light of demand conditions at the time of the contract, but recorded at the time of delivery which may be much later and with the background of different demand conditions.

The second strand of the administered price thesis concerns the ways in which demand and demand changes influence price changes are different in markets where prices are administered as compared with where prices are market-determined. At one level this could be seen as suggesting that there were some markets where price is determined by interplay of demand and supply, with price change determined by excess demand as discussed above, whilst in other markets firms set their prices in pursuit of their objectives. Thus the distinction would be between price-taking markets where prices were market-determined and price-making markets where prices were administered. Under the excess-demand approach, prices fall in response to falls in demand (leading to excess supply), whereas under the price-making approach prices may rise or fall in response to a fall in demand with any fall likely to be small. In the context of the 'thirties, infrequency of price change as well as the tendency towards lack of downward movement in price in response to low demand were seen as combining to prevent the downward adjustment of price thought necessary to promote economic recovery. Within a Keynesian approach to macro-economics prices have often been assumed fixed, with a downward rigidity of wages underpinning a downward rigidity of prices. In contrast, the administered price theses would tend to place the 'responsibility' for price rigidity in the product market rather than the labour market. Price rigidity in one market would tend to reinforce price rigidity in other markets, particularly those to which sales of output are made.

The precise nature of the administered price thesis has not always been clear, and this has presented acute problems when attempts have been made to test the thesis. A major difficulty is the determination of which industries are in the market determined price category and which in the administered-price category. Originally, Means (1935) categorised industries on the basis of frequency of price change (i.e. using the first strand of the administered price thesis) for the testing of the second part that in administered price industries, prices do not move with demand. Means (1972) also included in the market-determined price category those industries where there was an important input whose price was market-determined. On other occasions the categorisation has been in terms of the level of industrial concentration. For example, Weiss (1977) divides industries three ways based on four-firm concentration ratios. Many of the tests of the administered price thesis have been undertaken in terms of the price movements of different groups of industries for specified phases of the general business cycle, but without regard to differential movements in costs in the industries concerned. Thus the effects of differences in demand conditions and in cost changes may distort any underlying relationship between price change and concentration during phases of the trade cycle or may induce a phoney relationship, and these considerations add to the difficulties in interpreting the results from tests of the administered price thesis.

Most, if not all, testing of the administered price thesis has centred on the manufacturing sector. It can be argued that most industries in a developed economy, particularly the manufacturing sector, are oligopolistic and hence display some variety of administered pricing. Thus it is perhaps better to think in terms of the differences arising from variatons in the level of concentration on an essentially similar approach to pricing in different industries rather than contrast administered prices with market-determined prices. For the latter type of prices may be rare and arise from special features of the industries involved which make comparison with administered prices difficult. Thus we argue that most, if not all, industries will administer prices in the light of the objectives of the firms involved. We now turn to the question as to whether the level of concentration will influence the time path of prices.

From equation (13) above, which applied in the general oligopoly case, changes in price over a period can be seen as arising from changes in marginal costs and changes in the determinants of the mark-up. Provided that firms follow this short-run pricing rule, then we can analyse changes in price during, say, an upswing in economic activity via equation (13). The level of concentration may influence both the nature of changes in marginal costs as output changes and the determinants of the mark-up. For example, if oligopolists (or industries with high concentration) face decreasing marginal costs and competitive industries (or those with low concentration) face increasing marginal costs, then as output rose marginal costs and thereby price would fall for the first group and would rise for the second group. Here we would expect to find in a cross-section study an association between price changes and industrial structure. An argument in favour of this example would be that oligopolies tend to be located in capital-intensive industries with short-run declining costs, whereas competitive firms tend to be located in labour-intensive industries. Further, oligopolies may use excess capacity as an entry-barrier (Spence, 1977) which would generate declining marginal costs.

During a slump, oligopolies may be better able (than competitive firms) to prevent an outbreak of price-cutting. In terms of equation (13), this would mean a relatively higher value of α in a slump, and thus a higher price. Thus the argument is that during a slump industries with high level of concentration are able to maintain profit margins, which thus rise relative to those in less concentrated industries. In a boom, this position unwinds, with profit margins rising relatively in low concentration industries.

These types of argument suggest the hypothesis that during a boom, prices in concentrated industries (either as such or relative to cost of inputs) fall relative to prices in unconcentrated industries, and in a slump the former rise relative to the latter.

CONCLUSION

The behaviour of output prices is only part of the inflation story, but the price-making approach has a number of important implications for that story. When prices are administered by firms, then a reduction in price (relative to costs), which is what is involved in attempts to achieve a slow down in the overall rate of inflation, has a direct effect on the profits of the firms involved which firms are likely to try to resist through market and non-market channels. Since profits are relatively small in comparison with costs, particularly at the individual firm level, a moderate reduction in the rate of price increase below the rate of cost increases would have a large effect on profits. Thus, for example, with unit costs at 100 and unit profits at 20 giving a price of 120, if costs rose by 15 per cent and prices by 10 per cent then profits would be reduced by 30 per cent. If the reduction in inflation were pursued by deflationary macro-economic policies, then profits would be further reduced by falls in output. Some of these potential effect could be offset by negotiated reductions in cost increases, notably wages. Thus we expect to find that during attempts to reduce inflation whether by deflationary policies or the use of price and incomes policies, that reductions in price increases would follow behind reductions in cost increases, and much focus is placed on reducing wage increases.

There are many layers of production and distribution involved before a product reaches the final consumer. At each layer, as costs rose firms seek to maintain profits by raising prices. Further, at each stage labour costs and gross profits are relatively small proportions of total revenue. For UK manufacturing industry in 1978, it can be calculated from the Census of Production that wages and salaries were around $18\frac{1}{2}$ per cent of gross output, labour costs (including national insurance contributions) around $21\frac{1}{2}$ per cent and gross profits around $12\frac{1}{2}$ per cent. Thus once inflation is established within the system, its removal is particularly difficult. For at each stage, there is little to bite on in the sense that with input costs as a substantial proportion of revenue, a relatively large reduction in profits and/or wages is required for a relatively small reduction in the pace of inflation. The price-making approach also reminds us that the reduction of the rate of inflation is likely to involve some redistribution of income. If price rises fail to match cost prices, then profits fall, and if wage rises fail to match price rises then real wages fall. Thus rather than the anonymous market-operation on wages and prices via excess demand or supply, and no apparent reference made to gains or losses by particular groups, here we have groups seeking to maintain their income levels in face of inflation.

This chapter has sought to set out various equations which can be used to test the variety of approaches to price change determination. In the next chapter, we shall look at the competitive, excess demand variant and their performance empirically. Chapter 4 investigates the general equation derived from price-making considerations as well as the administered price thesis.

3 Excess Demand, Expectations and Price Changes

INTRODUCTION

In this chapter, we focus on the empirical evidence pertaining to theories of price change which give a central role to excess demand, set within the context of an essentially competitive market environment. We begin with a discussion of the problems which arise in testing such theories, particularly the measurement of crucial variables. After a brief survey of previous work in this area, we present a summary of the results of our own empirical investigation in this area for 40 British manufacturing industries over the period 1963 to 1975.

MEASUREMENT PROBLEMS

In seeking to test the various excess demand approaches to price change behaviour, it is necessary to measure price, excess demand and (sometimes) marginal costs. Further, measures of expected changes in price and costs are often required. In this section, we look in turn at the measurement problems involved with price, costs, excess demand and expectations.

The measures of price which was used in our empirical work were price indices from each industry included in our sample,[1] and this is a common practice. The price index relates to the prices charged by firms assigned to the industry in question, so that the question arises on the correspondence between industries and markets. An industry is generally defined in terms of either supply considerations such as the use of a similar production technique or major input, or demand considerations of goods which are close substitutes in consumption. It is often felt that supply, rather than demand, considerations dominate in the drawing of industrial boundaries for statistical purposes.[2] Even when demand considerations are used, the firms assigned to a particular industry may produce a wider range of goods than those which serve to define that industry (and firms assigned to other industries produce goods of the industry in question). Thus, in general, there may be only a loose correspondence between the statistical definition of industries (to which most data relate) and the notion of a market for goods which are close substitutes in demand (and in the limiting case of perfect competition a market for a homogeneous good). This discrepancy poses a problem throughout empirical work, which is greater for the excess demand approach than the others. In the other approaches, considered in the next chapter, prices, costs and output relate to the firms assigned to a particular industry. The behaviour of prices is seen as a firm-level activity (though perhaps influenced by actions of other firms in an industry), which can be averaged across firms in an industry to provide an industry average. At the industry level, the only way in which price can be measured is in index form, since in many of the price-making approaches differentiated products are involved. But, in the excess demand case, the problems are more severe. The theory of excess demand draws on the level of excess demand for a product in a particular market, and consequently the price should be the market, rather than the industry, price. The divergence between the boundaries of an industry and those of the corresponding market may create considerable difficulties for the testing of the excess demand theory.

There is the further question of the appropriate level of disaggregation which also illustrates a related problem with the excess demand approach. In the excess demand approach, as in perfect competition in general, it is assumed that there is a market for a well-defined homogeneous product, and there is no definitional problem over that product. But reality is not so simple. First, otherwise identical products delivered to different places at different times may be regarded for some purposes as the same product, but for other purposes as different products. Secondly, where there are elements of differentiation, a choice much be made in respect of the extent of difference between goods which will be tolerated whilst regarding them as the same product. Even within commodities such as wheat and coffee, there are different types such that it can be debated whether, for example, wheat should be treated as a product (and hence the wheat market discussed) or whether different types of wheat taken as the products (and so, the various markets for the various types of wheat discussed).

The consideration of products other than primary ones will generally involve product differentiation. The nature of the products made is then usually a decision for the firms involved to make, leading inevitably to product differentiation if only in terms of brand names and other minor differences. Products which are not closely linked to primary products are highly likely to involve product differentiation. For example, cars have to be designed and are not closely linked to a single primary product, so that differences in the product of different car firms is inevitable. Indeed, the production of identical cars may involve legal problems for the imitating firms. Thus the problem of product definition arises. Working from the demand angle, a product can be defined such that goods are grouped together which are close substitutes in terms of consumer demand. This means there may not be any obvious definition of products nor anything predetermined by nature. Rather the range of goods available, by influencing the substitutability and the cross-elasticities of demand between pairs of goods, would influence how products are defined.

This leads us back to a serious problem with the excess demand approach, namely that a theory heavily imbued with the concept of well-defined homogeneous product is applied to markets and industries involving differentiated heterogeneous products. As with the discussion on how prices change when all economic agents are price-takers, so here we have to take it that the forces (of excess demand) at work in perfect competition are also at work and having similar effects in situations of differentiated products without being able to formulate with any precision how that might come about.

We argued in Chapter 2 (p. 22) that the level of costs or cost changes which enter the Parkin (1975) excess demand approach (and costs do not enter the other approaches) relate to an index of input prices. Thus the measurement of these prices presents the problems associated with the construction of index numbers, but no other major problems.

The measurement of excess demand can be attempted through two routes. The first one is to seek proxies such as output (actual or relative to trend), capacity utilisation, stock changes for excess demand, whilst the second one is to try to use variables, such as relative prices, which are thought to determine demand and supply.

The problems of using various proxies for excess demand are discussed in terms of the use of deviations of output from trend as the proxy, but most of the discussion relates to all such measures. In Figure 3.1 demand and supply curves are drawn for a particular market, and output q^* taken as the trend level of output for the period in question. The particular position of q^* does not affect the line of argument, and some

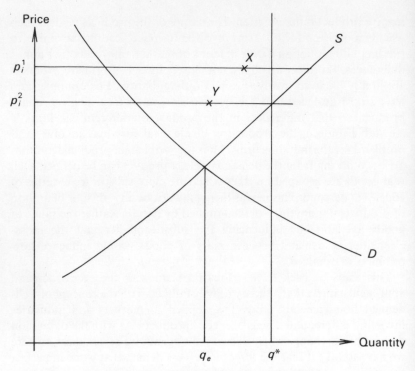

FIGURE 3.1   *Demand and supply configurations*

may wish to take the trend level of output as the equilibrium level (i.e. in terms of Figure 3.1 q_e and q^* would coincide). Let us first consider the case where all factors other than price and output in this market are held constant (including other prices, costs and the general level of demand). For prices to change then, excess demand has to be non-zero and the market out of equilibrium. The question then arises as to the level of output which will result under such conditions of disequilibrium. It is conventional to assume that actual output traded is the minimum of *ex ante* demand and supply. In which case for price above equilibrium actual output is determined by the demand function, whilst for price below equilibrium output is determined by the supply function. It can then be seen that for price above equilibrium as excess demand increases (i.e. excess supply decreases) with lower prices the term actual output minus trend output increases (since the extent to which actual output is below trend output declines). But for price below equilibrium, as demand increases (as price falls) output declines along the supply curve leaving the term actual output minus trend output declining. Thus in this case there is a positive relationship between excess demand and actual minus trend output for price above equilibrium, but a negative relationship for price below equilibrium. The only way in which a positive relationship between excess demand and actual minus trend output can be preserved is if it is asserted that the demand function always determines the amount traded.

It is clear that if the amount traded is not systematically determined in terms of the demand and supply functions then further problems arise.[3] For example, if at price p_i^1 in Figure 3.1 the amount traded corresponds to the point X and at price p_i^2 to point Y, then it can be seen that a rise in excess demand goes alongside a reduction in output (from X to Y) and a fall in the term actual minus trend output.

We next consider the impact of changes elsewhere in the economy beginning with changes in other prices. The supply curve depends on the input prices (c) and the demand curve on the general price level (p). The same proportionate rise of c and p would be expected to lead to the same rise in the equilibrium value of p_i, thereby maintaining the previous equilibrium relative prices.[4] But a change in the relationship between c and p would lead to changes in the equilibrium price and output. Further, the relative positions of the demand and supply curves would change. Suppose, for example, that the supply curve shifted to the right, thereby decreasing the level of excess demand corresponding to each price level. When price is above equilibrium, with the demand curve unchanged the amount of output traded would be the same before and after the supply curve shifted. Thus the same value of actual minus trend output would correspond to different levels of excess demand.

A major cause of shifts in the curves, particularly the demand curve, would in a Keynesian approach be shifts in the level of aggregate demand. Once again, if this is the case, the same level of output (and hence output minus trend) will correspond to different levels of excess demand.[5]

We conclude from this discussion that the use of proxies such as actual minus trend output are likely to be highly misleading indicators of the level of excess demand. However, given the popularity of such proxies in the formulation of excess demand approaches discussed in Chapter 2 (pp. 17–22) we make use of them below.

Another problem which arises in this context is that there is no story given as to how the market came to be in disequilibrium. If it is argued that the market has arrived in disequilibrium because the demand and/or supply curves have shifted, then problems similar to those which have just been discussed arise. Another possibility is that in an inflationary context with price changes based on expectations of other changes, the expectations which lead to a particular price change turned out to be incorrect thereby leading to the 'wrong' price change and price level. For example, suppose that c and p were both expected to rise by 10 per cent over the relevant period so that p_i was raised by 10 per cent. If c and p actually rose by 8 per cent, then p_i would be 2 per cent higher (relative to c and p) than intended. If p_i had originally been in equilibrium because of these expectational mistakes it would finish up out of equilibrium.

The second route for the measurement of excess demand is to write excess demand as $ED = D - S$ (demand minus supply), and then to postulate the nature of the demand and supply function. In our discussion of the Parkin (1975) approach in the previous chapter, it was seen that there demand was taken as a function of p_i/p and supply a function of c/p_i. Clearly in doing so a specific view of the determinants of demand and supply is taken, and in particular any role of the general level of demand, which Keynesians would stress, is omitted. Further, in general, since assumptions have to be made in this approach about the demand and supply functions, what is being tested is a combination of the excess demand approach and the assumptions about the demand and supply functions.

An alternative way of measuring excess demand would be to postulate a demand function of the $D = a_0 + a_1 (p_i/p) + a_2 Y$ where Y is a measure (such as consumer expenditure) of aggregate demand, with the supply function remaining as a function of c/p_i. This approach is adopted below (and results reported in Table 3.5).

Over time, productivity changes leading to shifts in the supply curve. In our empirical work below this is taken into account by using cost per unit of trend output.

Expectations about the course of future prices and costs play an important role in the monetarist explanation of inflation and in the related excess demand approach to price change behaviour. It was seen in the previous chapter that an element of non-continuous price adjustment has to be introduced to explain the presence of expectations, for if continuous adjustment were possible there would be no reason to look ahead. The measurement of expected price and cost changes present further problems. We follow the two main approaches to this problem in turn. First, expected price (and other changes) can be assumed to be formed adaptively. In broad terms this means that the expected price change relating to, say, time period t are based on adapting previous expectations concerning price change in the light of actual price changes. The expectations on the average value of x_t for the period t held during that period is labelled x_t^e. During the period there is some opportunity to observe the value of x, but the information on its value will not be complete until at least the period is ended. The experience of the past and previous expectations also help to inform current expectations. In the adaptive expectations scheme this can be expressed as $x_t^e = ax_{t-1}^e + (1-a)x_t$. The variable x could be price change, cost change or whatever. Adaptive expectations is a convenient assumption in that it permits the elimination of expectations for the price change equation as follows. If $\dot{p}_t = f(X_t) + b\dot{x}_t^e$ is the equation to be estimated then with the stochastic term entered we have:

$$\dot{p}_t = f(X_t) + b\dot{x}_t^e + u_t$$
$$\dot{p}_{t-1} = f(X_{t-1}) + b\dot{x}_{t-1}^e + u_{t-1}$$

Subtracting a times the second equation from the first one yields

$$\dot{p}_t - \dot{p}_{t-1} = f(X_t) - bf(X_{t-1}) + b(\dot{x}_t^e - a\dot{x}_{t-1}^e) + u_t - au_{t-1}$$

The term $(\dot{x}_t^e - \dot{x}_{t-1}^e)$ is then by assumption equal to $(1-a)x_{t-1}$ generating an equation which involves observable variables and hence the parameters (including a) can be estimated. The cost of using this technique is serial correlation induced into the equation. The stochastic term is $u_t - au_{t-1}$, and the correlation between successive stochastic terms is

$$E(u_t - au_{t-1})(u_{t-1} - au_{t-2}) = E(-au_{t-1}^2)$$

assuming that the original stochastic term was not serial correlated (so that, for example, $E(u_t u_{t-1}) = 0$). The estimation procedure adopted below makes allowance for this type of induced serial correlation.

Adaptive expectations can be viewed as essentially backward-looking. This is vividly illustrated by a process of successive substitution as follows. From $x_t^e = ax_{t-1}^e + (1-a)x_t$ and $x_{t-1}^e = ax_{t-2}^e + (1-a)x_{t-1}$

we can obtain $x_t^e = (1-a)x_t + a(1-a)x_{t-1} + (1-a)^2 x_{t-2}^2$

Continuing in this vein would lead to $x_t^e = (1-a)\sum_{j=0}^{\infty} a^j x_{t-j}$

which indicates current expectations as a weighted average of previous experience. As is well-known when x relates to a variable which is rising over time, then the adaptive expectations scheme, being based on past values, will persistently underestimate the future course of x. Thus if price inflation were accelerating then the adaptive expectations scheme would lead to under-estimation (or under-expectation) of the course of inflation.

This backward-looking aspect of adaptive expectations has proved a major weakness. The idea that expectations on a variable are formed in a forward-looking manner, and take into account information other than previous expectations and values of the variable has been a strong influence on the emergence of the concept of "rational" expectations. First advocated by Muth (1961), this concept involves the idea that all relevant information available to the economic agent is used in arriving at expectations about the value of economic variables, i.e. $x_t^e = E(x_t | I)$ where I represents the information available at the time when expectations are formed. Information is to be broadly interpretted to include knowledge of (relevant) economic theory, and of current values of economic variables.

It is further asserted that economic agents learn from experience and from economic theory so that, *on average*, their expectations about the future are correct, though in any particular time-period their expectations may be unfulfilled. This is expressed as $x_t^e = x_t + e_t$ where e_t is a random term with mean of zero. This formulation indicates that on average expectations concerning x_t are fulfilled, with some deviation (of e_t) between actual and expected in a specific time period.

In one sense the assumption of "rational" expectations solves the measurement of expectations problem easily, for simply the observed value can be used as a proxy for the expected value. Matters are, however, not quite so simple. First, the use of a proxy introduces (or reinforces) the problem of "errors in variables", which if present (as here) would lead to inconsistent estimates if ordinary least squares were used. Second, the use of such a proxy draws on only part of the "rational" expectations approach, namely that, on average, expectations are fulfilled. It does not incorporate the other part, namely that all relevant information is used. McCallum (1975) follows this latter approach. The full set of available information includes the relevant economic model and data on economic variables, and McCallum derives estimates of expected values by utilising the overall economic model. In the context of our estimation, following the second route would be close to impossible since in order to make an estimate of the price change equation for a single industry we would need to construct a complete model of the economy including the price change equations for the other industries involved. Thus we are drawn into using actual values as a proxy for expected values, whilst recognizing the "errors in variables" problem which this introduces.[6]

SURVEY OF PREVIOUS RESEARCH

One difficulty in surveying previous research is that often the estimated price change equations have drawn on features of both price-making and price-taking behaviour, sometimes under the euphemistic heading of an eclectic approach. For example, a term proxying excess demand or the level of demand is often added to a price equation which links price changes to cost changes based on some variant of mark-up pricing (e.g. Eckstein and Fromm, 1968). One problem with such an approach is that it would suggest that the maintenance of a given level of demand would generate continuing movements in price (relative to costs) leading to continuing rise or fall in profits. Further such equations are not developed from a coherent approach to price determination but the *ad hoc* listing of factors which have been suggested as influencing price changes.

Laidler and Parkin (1975) surveyed previous work in this area, and concluded that "papers by Rushdy and Lund (1967), McCallum (1970, 1974), Solow (1969) and Brechling (1972) all find positive and statistically significant coefficients on a variety of alternative excess demand variables. . . . In light of these studies, it seemed to be well established that excess demand exerted an upward pressure on prices independently of changes in factor prices and hence costs . . .".[7] Parkin (1977) (pp. 476–7) paraphrases this very closely, but then goes on to say that Godley and Nordhaus (1972) found from their estimation of several pricing equations some "which had negative excess demand coefficients, and used a variable representing demand pressure in the labor market rather than in the product market. Aside from its inappropriateness as an excess demand factor one would expect *a priori* that excess demand in the labor market, other things being equal, would lower the mark-up not raise it". However, Parkin fails to notice that many of the studies (i.e. Rushdy and Lund, McCallum, Solow) which he uses to justify the excess demand view of the world also use a demand for labour indicator for excess demand for output.

It is true as Laidler and Parkin state, that these studies found positive and statistically significant coefficients on excess demand terms. But they fail to report that these studies report many regression results, and only

some of them show positive coefficients. Further there are often
unsatisfactory features of these studies. Thus it cannot be said that the
conclusion of these studies was the upward pressure of excess demand on
prices was well established. Sylos-Labini (1979, pp. 158–9) reviews the
studies cited by Laidler and Parkin and finds their conclusion unjustified.

We begin our survey with the study of McCallum, which provides the
"pure" excess demand view. He begins with the view that $\Delta p_t = ae_t$ where
Δp_t is absolute change in price and e_t the level of excess demand for
output. But he amends this to changes in price depending on a
distributed lag function of e_t and its past values. Further the excess
demand for labour (d_t) is taken as a distributed lag function of
excess demand for output, beginning with e_{t-1}, i.e. a one period lag of
excess demand for labour behind that for output is introduced.
Manipulation yields:

$$\Delta p_t = ad_{t+1} + bd_t + c\Delta p_{t-1}$$

The absence of a constant term indicates that in the presence of zero
excess demand, prices would eventually stop changing, though in the
short-run prices would continue to change because of the presence of the
$c\Delta p_{t-1}$ term.

There is a number of peculiarities with this model. First, note that Δp_t
is the absolute change in price (i.e. $p_t - p_{t-1}$), rather than the proportionate change in price. This implies a kind of money illusion, in the
sense that for a given level of excess demand prices change by the same
absolute amount (i.e. the same number of pennies, cents or whatever),
even though price changes. Second, the change in price between time
$t-1$ and time t is related to product excess demand in time t, whereas it
would seem better to relate that change to demand in time $t-1$. This
problem is, in a sense, exacerbated when the move to excess demand for
labour is undertaken, in that the price change from time $t-1$ to t is
related to labour excess demand in time $t+1$. Third, if an excess demand
view of the world is pursued consistently then excess demand for labour
and excess demand for output are not positively related, nor are they
related with a lag. Walras' Law states that the sum of notional excess
demands is zero. When output and labour are the only goods then the
sum of excess demand for output plus excess demand for labour equals
zero, and hence when excess demand for output is positive, that for
labour will be negative. We can at this point refer back to the point made
by Parkin (1977) quoted above on the unsuitability of using a labour
market measure for the excess demand for output.

The results obtained by McCallum are a: 3.914 (standard error 1.06), b: − 3.200 (s.e. 1.14), c: 0.8136 (s.e. 0.096). One interpretation of these results would be that since the proposition $a + b = 0$ cannot be rejected on these figures changes in price are related to changes in demand and previous changes in price.

Brechling (1972) is also a "pure" excess demand exercise, with changes in price (measured by the GDP deflator) related to the level of excess demand proxied by the deviations of output from trend and previous price changes. We have already commented on the use of such proxies (pp. 43–5 above). The regression results indicate a *negative* and significant effect of the current level of excess demand on price change. Other regressions indicate that previous demand levels have a positive but non-significant effect on prices. When wholesale price index is used to measure prices, then the level of demand lagged two periods has a positive and significant effect. Thus the study of Brechling presents conflicting evidence. It is interesting to note that Brechling seeks to explain his negative effect of excess demand on price changes results by appealing to normal cost pricing arguments (see pp. 34–5 above).

Solow (1969) tested a variety of propositions, reflecting an eclectic approach, using quarterly and annual data for the United Kingdom and the United States. Whilst some of his regression results indicate positive and significant effects of the demand proxies on price changes, he does conclude that "my findings confirm the view frequently expressed (by Robert Neild and others) that the British price level is insensitive to demand pressures and primarily cost determined". And for the United States he says that "if I am to believe my own results – and if I do not, who will? – I have to conclude that, even in the United States, changes in the rate of inflation are not violently sensitive to changes in demand pressures". Indeed in many of the regressions reported for the United States, the demand proxy is not statistically significant.

The study of Rushdy and Lund (1967) seeks to test whether the inclusion of demand terms to an equation in which price changes are explained by cost changes is justified. This follows on the work of Neild (1963) which sought to establish that prices were based on trend costs (discussed pp. 65–6 below). The demand term used is again a demand for labour measure. Many results are presented but they can be broadly summarised as follows. The demand term is more often positive and significant when the longer period of 1950–60 is used rather than the shorter period 1953–60, and when changes in actual unit labour costs are used rather than changes in trend unit labour costs. It can be argued that the longer period includes the period of the Korean war with high levels of world-wide demand, and so the results for the shorter period are more representative of normal peace-time conditions. Further, the Neild thesis points to the use of trend labour costs rather than actual costs, and the general insignificance of demand terms when the former measure of labour costs is used lends support to the Neild thesis. It should also be noted that in the equations where actual unit labour costs are used there is evidence of substantial positive serial correlation. Thus, the estimated standard errors are biased downwards, narrowing the confidence interval around the estimated parameter and increasing the likelihood of concluding that the estimated parameter is significantly different from zero (Kmenta, 1971, p. 282).

A minimum conclusion from the above would be that the strong support for the excess demand view of price changes found by Laidler and Parkin (1975) should be discounted.

RESULTS OF OUR EMPIRICAL WORK

In this section we report on the results of our own empirical work in the area of excess demand price change equations. Drawing on the discussion in the previous chapter, we have selected equations for estimation, designed to reflect a range of views about the excess demand effects on price changes. These equations are:

$$\dot{p} = f(X) \tag{1}$$
$$\dot{p} = g(X) + \dot{p}^e \tag{2}$$
$$\dot{p} = a\dot{c}^e + (1-a)\dot{p}^e_w + cX \tag{3}$$
$$\dot{p} = h(D - S) \tag{4}$$

where $\dot{p}$ is quarterly rate of change of price, X is the deviation of output from trend (relative to trend), taken as a proxy for excess demand for output, $\dot{c}^e$ is expected change in costs, $\dot{p}^e_w$ expected change in wholesale prices, D demand for output and S supply of output. In equation (4) explicit demand and supply functions are considered as detailed below. The expectations in equation (2) are measured adaptively and in equation (3) by 'rational' expectations as well as by adaptive expectations.

The estimation of these equations was undertaken for each of 40 British manufacturing industries, using data specific to each industry over the period 1963 to 1975 using quarterly observations. A list of the industries involved is given in Appendix One. These 40 industries account for around one-third of manufacturing industry, and were chosen solely on the grounds of data availability. Some sectors, notably food, drink and tobacco are over-represented, whilst others, such as engineering are under-represented. In the case of engineering this arises in part from the difficulties of constructing price indices for industries where much of the output is customer-specific.

Almost all previous estimation of excess demand equations has proceeded at the aggregate level. One reason for estimation at the disaggregate level is that the problems which arise from aggregation (of price indices etc) are reduced. Another reason is that it is possible to explore the extent to which different industries price differ or in which the factors determining price changes vary. We return to this point in the final chapter.

The price change term is measured by the wholesale price index for the industry concerned. In general, these price series relate to quoted list prices, although this is not always the case. The cost series were constructed on a fixed (1968) weight basis, originally, for three separate items of costs, namely home produced inputs, foreign produced inputs and labour inputs. These separate cost indices are used in the next chapter, and details of their construction are given in Appendix II. These three cost series were combined, again using 1968 weights, into a single cost index. Output was measured by the index of industrial production for each industry, and the trend of output was estimated for an equation of the form $\log q_t = a + bt$ so that trend output $\bar{q}_t = e^{\hat{a}} \cdot e^{\hat{b}t}$ where $\hat{a}$ and $\hat{b}$ are the estimates of a and b respectively. The general price level (p_w) is measured by the wholesale price index.[8] Measures of aggregate demand used were consumers' real disposable income and industrial output. With the obvious exception of the aggregate price level and aggregate demand measures, all the other variables were measured specific to the industry concerned.

The number of regressions estimated for variants of the four equations listed above for each of 40 industries is clearly rather large. In our reporting of the regression results below, we present highly summarised accounts, focusing on the statistical significance of the estimated coefficients and whether the signs of the coefficients conform with the *a priori* notions.

The estimation technique used is single equation, though ordinary least squares, instrumental variable and maximum likelihood techniques are used as appropriate. In this context, simultaneous equation techniques are not employed since the impact of the dependent variable on the independent ones within the current time period is very small. At the aggregate level, there may be feedbacks of prices on wages within the current quarter, but this is unlikely at the level of disaggregation (3-digit) which is used in this study. There are lags between an industry's own price rise, the impact on costs in other industries, on the price level and on to wages and other costs which affect the industry in question. In this chapter, costs play a limited role anyway, but their importance will be greater in the next chapter.

In our estimation of the excess demand equations, seasonal dummies are included to capture any seasonal effects. Diagnostic checks for serial correlation were undertaken (as indicated below), and there appropriate allowance for serial correlation is made in the estimation procedure. In our presentation of results, statistical significance refers to the 5 per cent level (unless otherwise stated).

Our first batch of results relate to the linear version of equation (1) above (hereafter referred to as variant 1) and are summarised in Table 3.1. The rate of change of prices is approximated by $\dot{p}_t = (p_t - p_{t-1})/p_{t-1}$ (and other rates of change measured correspondingly). It seems then more appropriate to measure X by X_{t-1} than by X_t, i.e. excess demand at period $t-1$ is postulated to influence the change in price between period $t-1$ a period t. The empirical results reported in Table 3.1 refer to X_{t-1} as the excess demand theory. Estimation was also undertaken with X_t and log X_{t-1} as excess demand proxies. Those using X_{t-1} were somewhat better (from the view of the excess demand hypothesis) than the others. Other ways of calculating the trend output were considered, using moving eight-quarter and seventeen quarter averages (centred on the current quarter), but the results using the long run trend were again generally more favourable to the excess demand hypothesis. The method of estimation was the Cochranne-Orcutt technique allowing for up to fifth order serial correlation. For each industry, the regression result used in Table 3.1 was chosen as follows.

TABLE 3.1 *Summary of estimates of* $\dot{p}_{it} = a_0$
+ a_1 X_{t-1} + seasonals for 40 *industries*

	a_1
Number positive	25
of which statistically significant at 5 % level	11
Number negative	15
of which statistically significant at 5 % level	3

The equation was estimated with no allowance for serial correlation, then for first order, up to second order, third, fourth and then fifth order. A likelihood ratio test was employed to judge whether there was significant nth order serial correlation by comparing the equation with allowance for nth order with that which allowed for only $n-1$th order. In some cases the test would indicate that some of the middle orders of serial correlation were not significant but that higher orders were, and then the higher orders would be included.

In all cases there was evidence of some serial correlation. However, for 25 industries the serial correlation was of first order only (with no evidence of statistically significant higher orders of serial correlation), whilst in the other 15 the degree of serial correlation varied from second to fifth order.

The coefficient a_1 is clearly predicted to be positive, and is of that sign in 25 industries but negative in the remaining 15. When only the coefficients which are statistically significant (at the 5 per cent level) are taken into account, there are 11 industries in which excess demand as proxied by X_{it-1} plays a positive and statistically significant role. In Table 3.6 towards the end of the chapter, we list those 11 industries. The average value of a_1 implies that a 1 per cent rise in output relative to trend raises price change by 0.065 per cent per quarter, which can be contrasted with the average quarterly rate of change of prices of the order of 2 per cent in this period. The correlation between the actual and the predicted rate of change of prices calculated for the preferred equation for each industry was always above 0.0525 and averaged 0.751.

For equations (2) and (3), some view about the formation of expectations has to be taken. In the case of equation (2) (hereafter variant 2), "rational" expectations cannot be used, since that would lead to regressing $\dot{p}$ on itself, hence only adaptive expectations are used. For equation (3) both adaptive and "rational" expectations can be used, and these are referred to as variant 3a and 3b respectively.

For variant 2, we linearise it as $\dot{p}_{it} = a_0 + a_1 X_{t-1} + a_2 \dot{p}_{it}^e$ and with adaptive expectations taken as $\dot{p}_{it}^e = m\dot{p}_{it-1}^e + (1-m)\dot{p}_{it}$ using a technique outlined by Maddala (1977) we can obtain

$$\dot{p}_{it} = \sum_{j=0}^{t-1} m^j (a_0(1-m) + a_1 X_{it-j} - a_1 m X_{it-j-1})/h$$

$$+ \sum_{j=1}^{t-1} m^j \dot{p}_{it-j}(1-h)/h + m^t q_0/h + u_t/h$$

where $h = 1 - a_2(1-m)$ and q_0 is the outside sample value of $\dot{p}_{it} - u_t$ in

TABLE 3.2   *Summary of estimates of* $\dot{p}_{it} = a_0 + a_1 X_{it-1}$
$+ a_2 \dot{p}_{it}^e + seasonals + u_t$

	a_1
Positive	32
of which statistically significant at 5% level	9
Negative	8
of which statistically significant at 5% level	1
	$a_2 = 1$
Not rejected at 95% confidence level	20
Rejected at 95% confidence level	20

period 0. We obtained the maximum likelihood estimates for this equation by taking values of m from 0.05, 0.1 in 0.1 steps to 0.9, 095, and of a_2 from 0 to 1.6 in steps of 0.1 (with values such that $a_2 = 1/1 - m$ excluded), and by differentiating the likelihood function with respect to a_0, a_1, q_0 and σ^2 (the variance of u).

The results for this estimation are summarised in Table 3.2. The coefficient a_1 is predominantly positive, as predicted, but is significantly positive in 10 industries (i.e. a quarter of cases). The coefficient a_2 is predicted to be unity, and in 20 cases, this prediction was not rejected by the estimated equation. It can be noted that there was no case where the estimated value of a_2 exceeded unity. There were two industries in which a_1 was positive and significant and a_2 was not significantly different from unity, and it could be said that in those two industries this version "worked".

The average degree of correlation between actual and predicted values of the rate of price change was 0.699. However, in all cases there was evidence (based on number of sign changes of the residuals (Geary 1970)) of positive serial correlation.

The model based on Parkin (1975) is examined first with the adaptive expectations mechanism, and then with rational expectations. We have three equations:-

$$\dot{p}_{it} = d_0 + d_1 X_{it-1} + d_2 \dot{c}_{it}^e + d_3 \dot{p}_{wt}^e + u_t$$
$$\dot{c}_{it}^e = m\dot{c}_{it-1}^e + (1-m)\dot{c}_{it}$$
$$\dot{p}_{wt}^e = n\dot{p}_{wt-1}^e + (1-n)\dot{p}_{wt}$$

Again using the technique suggested by Maddala (1977), we arrive at

$$\dot{p}_{it} = d_0(1 - A_t(m, n) - B_t(m, n)) + A_t(m, n)q_0 + B(m, n)q_{-1}$$
$$+ \sum_{r=1}^{t-1} (m^r - n^r).Z_{t-r-1}/(m-n) + u_t$$

where $A_t(m, n) = (m^{t+1} - n^{t+1})/(m-n)$, $B_t(m, n) = -mnA_{t-1}(m, n)$,
$Z_t = d_1(X_{it-1} - (m+n)X_{it-2} + mnX_{it-3}) + d_2(1-m)(\dot{c}_{it} - n\dot{c}_{it-1})$
$+ d_3(1-n).(\dot{p}_{wt} - n\dot{p}_{wt-1})$

and q_0, q_{-1} are the outside sample values of $\dot{p}_{it} - u_t$ in periods 0 and -1. We write this equation, with obvious notation as $\dot{p}_{it} = Q_t + u_t$. The maximum likelihood estimates were obtained by minimising $S(m, n) = \sum_t (p_{it} - Q_t)^2$ with respect to $d_0, d_1, d_2, d_3, q_0, q_{-1}$ for different values of m and n ($m \neq n$) between 0 and 1.

The grid values used for m and n were 0.05, 0.1 by tenths to 0.9, and 0.95. The estimated asymptotic variances were obtained from the diagonal elements of $(-\partial^2 L/\partial\theta_i\partial\theta_j)^{-1}$ where L is the log likelihood function and θ_i the parameters of the function. The equation was estimated without and then with the constraint $d_2 + d_3 = 1$ imposed. The difference between the values of the log likelihood functions in the two instances multiplied by minus 2 is distributed as a χ^2 with 1 degree of freedom. Of the 40 industries for which the equations were estimated, the constraint was rejected at the 95 per cent confidence level in 13 industries. In reporting the results below, we have used the estimates for the equation where the constraint is imposed when that constraint is not rejected for that industry; otherwise the unconstrained version is used.

In Table 3.3 a summary of the results is given. It can be seen that the excess demand term has a positive coefficient in nearly three-quarters of the industries, but in only just under half of these industries is it statistically significant. Within the group of industries for which the constraint is not rejected, 11 of them have an estimated value which is outside the permissible range. In 8 cases, the value of d_2 is negative and in all those cases the coefficient is different from zero in a statistically significant degree. In the three other cases, the coefficient is greater than unity in a statistically significant manner, implying that d_3 is negative.

If we take those industries in which the constraint is not rejected, in which the excess demand term has a positive and statistically significant coefficient and in which d_2 does not lie outside the range zero to one in a statistically significant manner, then we have nine industries in which it could be argued that the Parkin excess demand/expectations theory of price change holds.

TABLE 3.3 *Summary of estimates of*
$$\dot{p}_{it} = d_0 + d_1 X_{it-1} + d_2 \dot{c}_{it}^e + d_3 \dot{p}_{wt}^e + seasonals + u_t$$
adaptive expectations

		of which statistically significant at 5% level
Sign of d_1		
Positive	29	15
Negative	11	4
Industries in which $d_2 + d_3 = 1$ accepted		
Value of d_2 *coefficient*		
Negative to a statistically significant extent	8	
Negative but not to a statistically significant extent	0	
Positive but not to a statistically significant extent	3	
Positive to a statistically significant extent	16	
of which greater than unity to a statistically significant extent	3	
Industries in which $d_2 + d_3 = 1$ constraint rejected	13	

Finally, we have to record that for this variant there is positive serial correlation indicated in every estimate of this equation. Using the Geary (1970) sign test, on average there are 9 sign changes (out of a possible 46), which indicates significant positive serial correlation.

The second approach to the generation of expectations is that of "rational" expectations, which as indicated above allows us to substitute $x_t + u_t$ for x_t^e. The "errors in variable" problem thereby induced is overcome by using instrumental variable estimation. The equation estimated is:

$$\dot{p}_{it} = d_0 + d_1 X_{it-1} + d_2 \dot{c}_{it} + d_3 \dot{p}_{wt} + u_t + seasonals,$$

and the instruments are the constant, seasonals, X_{it-1}, X_{it-2}, X_{it-3}, $\dot{c}_{it-1}, \dot{c}_{it-2}, \dot{c}_{it-3}, \dot{p}_{wt-1}, \dot{p}_{wt-2}, \dot{p}_{wt-3}$. In all but one case based on the test proposed by Sargan (1964) and Godfrey (1972), the instruments were judged to be suitable and not related to the error term.

The equation was first estimated as indicated above, and then with the constraint $d_2 + d_3 = 1$ imposed, using the same set of instruments. In order to investigate whether the constraint was consistent with the data, the statistic $\dfrac{\phi_R - \phi_{UR}}{\sigma_{UR}^2}$ was computed

where $\phi = \mathbf{a}(X_\rho)' \mathbf{Z}(\mathbf{Z}'\mathbf{Z})^{-1} \mathbf{Z}'(X_\rho)\mathbf{a}'$, where $\mathbf{a}$ is the vector of estimated coefficients, X_ρ the matrix of elements $(x_{it} - \rho_1 x_{it-1})$, where x is the vector of independent variables, and Z the matrix of instruments, for the restricted and unrestricted cases respectively, and σ_{UR}^2 is the estimated standard error of the unrestricted regression. This is distributed asymptotically as a χ^2 distribution with degrees of freedom equal to the number of constraints imposed (in this case, one).

The estimation procedure allowed for up to fourth order autocorrelation, and the appropriate degree of autocorrelation was determined with reference to the unconstrained equation. The test described above was then applied to make a comparison between the unconstrained equation with the degree of autocorrelation so determined and the constrained version with the same degree of autocorrelation. The constraint was rejected in eight industries (out of 40). The results for this approach are summarised in Table 3.4.

Employing similar criteria to those used above for the variant 3a, there are four industries for which the 'rational' expectations/excess demand hypothesis can be said to hold.

For the estimation of equation (4), we have to specify the nature of the demand and supply functions. We use the following

$$D_Q(t) = a_0 + a_1 Y_t + a_2 (p_{it}/p_{wt})$$
$$S_Q(t) = a_3 + a_4 (c_{it}/p_{it})$$

TABLE 3.4 *Summary of estimates of*
$$\dot{p}_{it} = d_0 + d_1 X_{it-1} + d_2 \dot{c}_{it}^e + d_3 \dot{p}_{wt}^e + seasonals + u_t$$
'Rational' expectations

		of which statistically significant at 5% level
Sign of Positive	24	6
Negative	16	3
Industries in which $d_2 + d_3 = 1$ constraint accepted	32	
In those industries, value of d_2		
Negative and statistically significant	0	
Negative but not statistically significant	11	
Positive but not statistically significant	13	
Positive and statistically significant	8	
of which greater the unity to a statistically significant extent	1	
Industries in which $d_2 + d_3 = 1$ constraint rejected	8	

where Y_t is a measure of aggregate demand. As we have already argued, the involvement of an aggregate demand term corresponds to a Keynesian position and a neo-classical position would point towards $a_1 = 0$. From $\dot{p}_{it} = f(D_Q(t-1) - S_Q(t-1))$ with a linear form of f, we can arrive at an equation of the form[9]

$$\dot{p}_{it} = b_0 + b_1 Y_{t-1} + b_2 (p_{it-1}/p_{wt-1}) + b_3 (c_{it-1}/p_{it-1})$$

where it is postulated that $b_1 > 0$ (a Keynesian position) or $b_1 = 0$ (a neo-classical position), $b_2 < 0$ and $b_3 > 0$.

Disposable income and industrial output were both used as indicators of aggregate demand. The use of disposable income yields results slightly more favourable to the maintained hypothesis than the use of industrial output does. For the sake of brevity only the results derived from the use of disposable income are presented here. In Table 3.5, we summarise those results. The estimated coefficients have, in general, the predicted sign and for the three coefficients reported an average of 80 per cent have the predicted sign, with just over half of those 'correct' signs are statistically significant (at the 5 per cent level).

TABLE 3.5　*Summary of estimates of*
$$\dot{p}_{it} = b_0 + b_1 Y_{t-1} + b_2 p_{it-1}/p_{wt-1} + b_3 c_{it-1}/p_{it-1} + seasonals + u_t$$

	b_1	b_2	b_3
Predicted sign	+	−	+
Number positive	34	10	32
of which significant at 5% level	16	1	17
Number negative	6	30	8
of which significant at 5% level	2	14	1

The correlation between actual and predicted value averaged 0.826 and was above 0.59 in all industries (with slightly fewer figures recorded for industrial output used as the aggregate demand indicator.) The degree of serial correlation was indicated as zero in six industries, first order in 11, second order in four, third order in two, fourth order in 11 and fifth order in the remaining six.

The predicted sign pattern is found in 18 industries, and could not be rejected in a total of 35 industries. But in only two industries were the coefficients of the predicted sign and all statistically significant from zero.

In Table 3.6 we have tried to summarise the results for each of five variants of the excess demand/expectations hypothesis discussed in detail above, in terms of the industries for which that variant "works".

TABLE 3.6 *Summary of industries for which variants of excess demand/expectations hypotheses "works"*

Variant	Industry number*	Total
1	1, 3, 5, 17, 24, 27, 32, 33, 37, 38, 41	11
2	33, 34	2
3a	1, 5, 9, 17, 24, 27, 32, 33, 37	9
3b	1, 5, 16, 21	4
4	2, 11, 12, 21, 29,[+] 35, 36,[+] 41	8

NOTES
* For list of industry number, see Appendix One
[+] For these industries, all three coefficients statistically significant

The criteria applied have to vary between the five variants, and may in some sense be more stringent for some variants than for others. For variant 1 we have listed those industries for which the coefficient of X_{t-1} is positive and statistically significant. For variant 2, we include those industries for which the coefficient of X_{t-1} is positive to a statistically significant extent and for which the hypothesis that $a_2 = 1$ cannot be rejected at the 95 per cent level. For variants 3a and 3b, inclusion is based upon a positive and significant coefficient on X_{t-1}, the non-rejection of the constraint $d_2 + d_3 = 1$ and d_2 not falling outside the range 0 to 1 to a significant extent. In the case of variant 4 we list those industries for which we can accept that at the 95 per cent level two at least of the coefficients b_1, b_2 and b_3 are of the predicted sign, and that for the remaining coefficient (if any) we cannot reject the view that the estimated coefficient is of the predicted sign.

These five variants are not independent, and the term X_{it-1} appears as an explanatory variable in four of them. However, between the five variants there are 14 industries which appear once, six industries which appear twice, and two industries which appear three times. But there are 21 industries for which none of the five variants appear to "work" (and this figure would be unchanged if the alternative version to variant two based on industrial output as aggregate demand indicator were added).

The major interest of our investigation is the question of the influence of a change in demand on the rate of change of prices. In the variants considered above, on balance, an increase in (excess) demand leads to an increase in the rate of price change. But there is often a significant minority of industries where the effect of a demand change is apparently to reduce the rate of change of prices. Over all, the quantitative aspect of a reduction of excess demand on rate of price change is small. In the first variant discussed, for example, a 1 per cent reduction in output relative to trend (which is the measure of excess demand) leads, on average, to a reduction in price changes of 0.086 per cent.

Our study indicates that the pattern of price changes differs across industries in a number of respects. From Table 3.6, it can be seen that which, if any, of the excess demand hypotheses are found acceptable varies between industries. Further, the extent of serial correlation and the role of seasonal dummies also vary between industries.

CONCLUSION

We have seen that the empirical investigation of the excess demand view of price change is fraught with difficulties arising from measurement problems and varying specifications of the excess demand approach. Our brief survey of previous work taken together with the results of our own investigations do not appear to lend much support to the excess demand approach.

4 Cost Changes, Demand Changes and Price Changes

INTRODUCTION

This chapter seeks to answer (if only provisionally) a number of questions thrown up by the earlier discussion. In Chapter 2 we drew a sharp distinction between price-taking theories in which the level of excess demand was a key factor in determining price changes and price-making theories in which changes in the level of demand and in costs were amongst the key factors. In Chapter 3 we reviewed and presented evidence on the excess demand approach. In this chapter, we seek answers to the questions of whether changes in demand do, in practice, influence price changes and the quantitative importance of any such influences, and of the effect of cost changes on price changes. For this latter question we wish to investigate the quantitative importance of different types of costs (e.g. labour costs relative to material input costs), and the length of lags between cost changes and price changes.[1] Another question is that of the influence of industrial structure (particularly concentration) on the process of price change. Under this head, we would wish to look at questions of the influence of industrial structure on price flexibility, as well as on the effects of cost and demand changes on price changes. We can also to some extent pursue the question of whether industries pursue similar price change policies (in the sense of responding to cost and demand changes in the same way and to the same extent). We would expect that since different industries have different cost structures (e.g. proportion of costs arising from labour differ), the coefficients on the various cost changes terms would differ. This feature may by itself create aggregation problems and we return to that question in the last chapter.

In the next sections we focus on studies which have related price changes to cost and demand conditions, first surveying previous work and then reporting on the results of our own work. In the final sections, we focus on studies which have investigated the role of industrial structure on price change, although inevitably many of those studies also bear on the question of the effects of cost and demand changes on price changes.

SURVEY OF PREVIOUS WORK

Studies of price determination and price change can be divided into two broad groups. The first group is those which have used a case study/interview approach, whilst the second group contains those which are econometric-based.

The interview/case study approach has usually been used with firms which could be said to administer prices. Thus since the focus of these studies has often been on questions of how businesses determine prices, it is very likely that only those businesses which believe that there is a decision about price to be made are involved. In those markets where firms believe that they are price-takers, then there is no price decision to be made. Thus the proposition that excess demand leads to price changes cannot really be tested through the case study approach (or at least not through a survey of previous case studies). Indeed, it can be argued that it is an underlying assumption of most case studies on price determination that prices are not set through the anonymous operation of demand and supply in a competitive market.

Many of the case studies on price determination have been concerned with questions of whether the mark-up of price over costs is constant or varies with the level of demand, the exact nature of the costs which are marked-up and whether costs are constant with respect to output.

Silberston (1970) concluded his survey of empirical studies on pricing by saying that "full cost (pricing) can be given a mark of beta query plus, but no more than this, since there are so many marginalist and behavioural qualifications. It seems clear that the *procedure* of calculating prices very often starts with an average-cost type calculation, but the qualifications that arise are concerned with the next stages of the process, including the exact method by which full costs are calculated".

Hay and Morris (1979) indicate that their "main conclusion is that increases in demand do appear to have the impact on margins predicted (if the former is interpretted as a fall in the elasticity of demand), but the sensitivity of margins (as opposed to prices) to cost changes is not so clear. Finally, this summary supports the initial point that it is dangerous to generalise about firms' pricing procedure".

These surveys indicate two important points. First, the debate is around whether the price-cost margin is sensitive to the level of demand. Secondly, that there is a wide variety of pricing procedures used so that a general conclusion is not warranted.

We begin our survey of econometric price equations by looking at those studies which have emphasised the role of costs and argued that demand and output changes can be ignored in terms of price changes.

Neild (1963) examines equations which explain the price level in terms of unit costs for British manufacturing industry (excluding food, drink and tobacco) over the period 1950 to 1960 (and sub-period 1953 to 1960 chosen to exclude the effects of the Korean war). After allowing for the lagged effects of costs on price, he arrives at an equation of the form

$$p = b_0 + b_1 w + b_2 m + b_3 m_{-1} + b_4 m_{-2} + b_5 p_{-1} \tag{1}$$

where w is a measure of unit labour costs and m an index of material input prices. Neild uses three measures *of* w, namely:

(i) actual unit labour costs;
(ii) labour costs divided by trend level of output, where trend growth of output is assumed to be $2\frac{1}{2}$ per cent per annum;
(iii) labour costs divided by trend output, where the growth rate is not exogeneously fixed but determined by the regression.

The hypothesis advanced by Neild is that firms base prices on trend labour costs rather than actual labour costs. His results (p. 13) confirm his view with the estimated value of b_1 being statistically non-significant where definition (i) is used, but statistically significant and positive when definitions (ii) or (iii) are used. These equations also appear to have considerable explanatory power, when it is indicated that the R^2 between the actual and predicted values of price changes $(p - p_{-1})$ is generally over 0.8.

The influence of demand is examined in the following manner. It is argued that since a given level of excess demand would be associated with a change in price, the level of prices would be linked with the cumulative value of excess demand. In view of our earlier discussion, this is an unsatisfactory mix of competitive pricing (reflected in linking excess demand and price changes) and oligopolistic pricing (reflected in cost-plus pricing). Further, the index of excess demand is a measure of excess demand for labour, with the problems which were noted in the previous chapter (see p. 50 above). We can merely note Neild's conclusion that demand "added nothing useful to the explanation of prices".

In the previous chapter, we discussed the critique of Neild made by Rushdy and Lund (1967), interpretting the latter study as one which could throw light on the role of excess demand. We noted there that their results would be interpretted as tending to support Neild's conclusion. Godley and Nordhaus (1972) explored a similar view (as indicated in Chapter 2 p. 35). They carried out a pilot study for all non-food industries, which was followed by Coutts, Godley and Nordhaus (1978) in which the price behaviour of seven broad industry groups four over the period 1957–73 and three over 1963–73 were examined. They normalise costs to remove the effects of changes in hours worked and in labour productivity during the course of the business cycle. These changes arc assumed to be regarded as reversible by the firm and discounted when price decisions are made. The determination of the basic hourly rate of earnings (for the normal length of working week) is not adjusted for any labour market demand effects. Similarly, the normalised cost of material inputs is taken as their actual cost, and thereby it is assumed that the ratio of material inputs to output does not vary (with output) and that variations in input prices is accepted as permanent. After the normalisation of unit labour costs, a predicted price is derived based on the postulate that price is a constant mark-up over these normalised costs.[2] The "normal price" hypothesis is tested by examining the estimated equation:

$$\Delta \log p_t = a_0 + a_1 \Delta \log \hat{p}_t + u_t \tag{2}$$

where p_t is actual price, $\hat{p}_t$ is the predicted price described above, and Δ denotes first difference in the appropriate variable and $\Delta \log p_t$ is for small price changes approximately equal to the proportionate rate of change of p. The version of the normal price hypothesis which postulates price as a constant mark-up over normalised cost would lead to the prediction of $a_1 = 1$ in the above equation. But a modified version which argues that the mark-up is unaffected by demand factors but can be changed by other factors could lead to a value of a_1 different from unity. In the British context, with declining profitability over the sample period, a value of a_1 less than unity could be anticipated. Coutts, Godley and Nordhaus argue that since normalised costs cannot be measured with complete accuracy, and that tax changes and the imposition of price control are not reflected in this equation then the estimated coefficient a_1 will be biased downwards.

On a quarterly basis, using the average cost version, normal prices are able to "explain" over 50 per cent of changes in actual prices, with the exception of one industry (electrical engineering) where the explanatory power falls to 32 per cent.[3] Given that it is quarter to quarter changes in price which are being explained, this can be regarded as a reasonable result. With the average cost version, it is not possible from their book to say how long the average lag of price behind cost is. It can be noted, however, that the production period averages between six and ten months (depending on precise assumptions made).

The crucial question remains of the influence of demand factors on prices. Coutts, Godley and Nordhaus examine the influence of demand by adding various measures of demand pressures to equation (2) and testing for the statistical significance of the demand pressure terms. Their preferred option is the addition of the term $\Delta \log X/XN$ (current and lagged) where X is actual output and XN normal output.[4] Our discussions in Chapter 2 (e.g. pp. 22–36) would indicate that this is an appropriate measure of demand pressure in the context of an oligopolistic pricing model. Laidler and Parkin (1975) comment on the original work of Godley and Nordhaus (1972) that "this is an incorrect specification", and argue that price change should be related to the level of excess demand. We have explored this question at length in Chapter 2, and our discussion there indicates a distinction between competitive price theory (where price changes are linked to excess demand) and oligopolistic theory (where price changes are linked to cost changes and demand changes), and to a distinction between excess demand and demand pressures.

However, Coutts, Godley and Nordhaus do also test for the inclusion of a level of demand term, i.e. add $\log X/XN$ to equation 2. We have noted above (pp. 43–5) the shortcomings of this measure as a proxy for excess demand.

In sum, 252 equations were estimated in the search for demand influences and in seven of those demand influences were judged to be positive and significant whilst in 16 these influences were negative and significant.[5] Of the 84 equations where the level of demand was tested for influence on changes in price, in only three was the influence judged to be positive and significant and in four the influence was judged to be negative and significant. Given that significance is being judged at the 5 per cent level, these figures are not substantially different from those one would anticipate if there were no effect of demand on price changes.

Two comments on the work of Coutts, Godley and Nordhaus. First, they have not entirely purged their cost series of possible demand influences. It was noted that their adjustments to unit labour costs only took account of changes in hours worked (and their impact on hourly earnings) and in labour productivity. Thus, changes in the general level of wages and also changes in material input prices which resulted from changes in the general level of demand would remain. Secondly, because they start from the hypothesis that it is normalised costs which determine prices, the econometric tests of the influence of demand are inevitably unsatisfactory. The theory rules out the influence of demand and so gives no indication of the channels through which demand influences would affect price changes, and thus no indication of how the presence of demand influences should be modelled.

RESULTS OF OUR EMPIRICAL WORK

Our approach indicates how demand influences operate in terms of changes in demand, and through the effect of changes in demand and output on costs (average or marginal) and the mark-up. We begin with the most general form whereby price changes are related to cost changes, output changes as well as a function of output, and test for the acceptability of restrictions imposed by the removal of certain terms (eg. cost changes in the past, output changes). Before reporting the results of our approach, we need to specify it more exactly.

In Chapter 2 we argued that price change equations based on the speedy adjustment of prices in circumstances of price-making behaviour lead to a general equation of the form:

$$\dot{p} = a.\dot{v} + h(q)\dot{q} \tag{3}$$

where the sum of the terms of the a-vector is unity, v is vector of input prices, q output.

Equations of this general type have often been estimated, sometimes with the omission of the equivalent of the $h(q)\dot{q}$ term, sometimes with the function related to the level of output only included (eg. capacity utilisation) rather than one involving the rate of change of output. Insofaras equations of this type are derived from price-making behaviour, they face the common problem that price and output are joint decision variables of the firms involved. Thus the equation does not indicate a causal relationship between output change and price change, but rather a connection between the two change variables derived from a decision taken by the firms. In the case of the price-taking behaviour, the view is that excess demand *causes* price changes and that the time sequence is that of excess demand followed by price changes. However, as price change the level of excess demand will change so that there may be some feed-back of price change on excess demand within the time period being used. In the price-making case, the firms face a level of demand which is divided up into prices and output depending on the decisions taken by the firms. Thus an alternative approach is to link directly price changes to changes in demand, rather than indirectly via changes in output. We return to this below.

We need to take account of joint determination of $\dot{p}$ and $\dot{q}$, in the estimation of equation 3. It would then be anticipated that random errors in $\dot{p}$ and random errors in $\dot{q}$ will be associated in that a higher than average predicted rise in output would, via the demand function, lead to a lower than average rise in price. In terms of an estimated equation of the form:

$$\dot{p} = a \cdot \dot{u} + h(q)\dot{q} + u \tag{3'}$$

there would be a predicted correlation between $\dot{q}$ and u. This leads to inconsistent estimates if the ordinary least squares technique is used. The problem can be treated as equivalent to an "errors-in-variable" problem, and hence we use instrumental variable estimation.

Most previous work in testing for the presence of demand effects in terms of an equation like (3) have not taken account of this point, which leaves open the possibility that their estimates are inconsistent (in the statistical sense).

The view that price changes are only determined by cost changes can be tested by examining whether $h(q) \equiv 0$. The case where the effect of demand changes (through output changes) are constant with respect to the level of output corresponds to the case where $h(q) = c$ (a constant), and this has been the usual case examined. The effect of changes of output may increase as capacity is approached and this can be reflected by $h(q) = c + dq$. Finally, we can allow for the possibility that initially $h(q)$ is negative (reflecting declining costs) and later it is positive as output increases by the use of a quadratic function $h(q) = c + dq + eq^2$. The use of this function could also capture the possibility of the effects of output change rise sharply as output approaches capacity utilisation. In sum them we have four versions of the $h(q)$ function, and we will estimate equation (3) for each of the four versions in turn.

The logic of profit maximisation in conjunction with the notion of opportunity cost would indicate that firms would use replacement cost of inputs in their pricing process, and hence only current cost changes would be included in the price change equation. However, the production process in manufacturing industries takes considerable amount of time with inputs entering at various states of the process. Coutts, Godley and Nordhaus (1978) discuss this in some detail. Okun (1981) (p. 155–69) suggests a number of reasons why firms in practice would not be either able or willing to follow replacement cost pricing, which include problems of determining the replacement cost of an input. Firms may adopt various rules of thumb to cope with those problems, which would bring in elements of historic cost, and thereby lagged cost changes into the price change equation.

The general equation (3) was derived from theories of the firm other than profit maximisation. And if, for example, a sales maximising firm is required by its shareholders to earn a particular level of profits measured in historic cost terms, then the managers might well base their pricing decisions on historic cost in seeking to achieve the profits target. Within the same industry, firms may use a variety of notions of costs in arriving at their pricing decisions. Thus we allow for these considerations by including a variety of lagged cost changes, and then test for the appropriateness of their inclusion. Specifically in the work reported above, we allowed for the following combinations of lagged cost changes. The lags on changes in cost of domestically produced inputs, on foreign produced inputs and on labour input were one of (i) (0, 0, 0) respectively, (ii) (2, 2, 2) and (iii) (4, 4, 2). From previous estimation, we believe that, these sets of lags cover the spectrum reasonably well. It was thought necessary to restrict the number of possible sets of lagged cost changes, partly to reduce the possibility of finding spurious significance and partly to make the estimation procedure manageable bearing in mind that 40 industries are involved.

Thus from the output function we have four choices and from the cost change terms we use three choices, and the combination of these alternatives leads to twelve versions of equation 3. The equation estimated is then in its most general form:

$$\dot{p}_t = \alpha_0 + \alpha_1 S_{1t} + \alpha_2 S_{2t} + \alpha_3 S_{3t} + \sum_{i=0}^{n_h} \beta_i \dot{h}_{t-i} + \sum_{i=0}^{n_f} \gamma_i \dot{f}_{t-i}$$

$$+ \sum_{i=0}^{n_l} \delta_i \dot{l}_{t-i} + (\sigma_1 + \sigma_2 q_{t-1} + \sigma_3 q_{t-1}^2)\dot{q}_t + u_t \qquad (4)$$

where S_{kt} ($k = 1, 2, 3$) are seasonal dummies.

Seasonal dummies are included since the data are not seasonal adjusted and this allows for any seasonal effects which are likely to be most pronounced in the output and output change terms. The change in a variable is approximated by $(x_t - x_{t-1})/x_{t-1}$ expressed as a percentage. With this approximation involving the change from period $t-1$ to period t it is appropriate to use the level of output at time $t-1$, rather than at time t, in the estimated equation.

The estimation technique here was instrumental variables, with instruments $\dot{h}_{t-j}, \dot{f}_{t-j}, \ l_{t-j} (j = 0, 1, \ldots, 6)$ constant term and seasonal dummies in all cases. We tested to see whether these instruments were acceptable in the sense of being uncorrelated, with the error term by means of χ^2 test (Chatterji and Wickens, 1981), and in all cases there was no significant association between the instruments and the error term.

The alternative forms of the output function can be viewed as more or less restrictive, and thus, for a given set of cost change terms, we can test as between any two alternatives for the restriction implied by the more restrictive version. For example, as between the linear version and the quadratic version of $h(q)$, we would test (as indicated below) for the acceptability of the restriction that $\sigma_3 = 0$. Similarly for the alternatives of the cost change terms.

The way in which we approached finding the appropriate set of cost change lags and output function is as follows. When a less general version nested within a more general version contains fewer cost change terms *and* less output terms then we can test for the acceptance of the implied restrictions of the less general version (*vis-à-vis* the more general version) in a number of ways. We could test first for the acceptability of dropping the cost change term, and then for dropping the output term, or vice versa, or to test for dropping both terms together. When we can move from the most general terms (four cost lags, quadratic output function) to another version, say, X such that by whatever order we impose the various restrictions they were not rejected, and when any further restrictions imposed on X (to lead to a less general version) were rejected then version X becomes the "preferred version".

However, it is not always possible to find a version X which fits that description. We may find that the restrictions implied by a move to version Y and those involved in a move to version Z were rejected, but Y and Z were non-nested and the imposition of further restrictions on either of them were rejected (and in particular a move to the version nested within both of them is rejected). In such a case, we report both Y and Z as joint "preferred versions".[6]

The test applied for acceptance or rejection of the restriction was the test described in the previous chapter (p. 58).

The estimation of the twelve variations of equation 1 was made without any allowance for serial correlation. We applied a specification test, based on a Lagrange multiplier approach (Breusch and Godfrey 1981), or first- and fourth-order serial correlation in the most general version, and in no case was significant serial correlation detected.[7]

The inference of the effects of demand changes on price changes from the coefficient (which may vary with output) on output change has been indicated above in Chapter 2 (pp. 26–7), and from there we can see that usually a positive coefficient on $\dot{q}$ implies positive coefficient on demand changes.

The nature of the preferred version of equation (4) for each of the 40 industries is indicated in Table 4.1. We have referred to the industries by our numbering system, and a list of the industries with their numbers is given in Appendix I. There are eight industries in which our procedure did not yield a unique preferred version, but two non-nested versions. The main figures in Table 4.1 refer to the 32 industries where there was a unique preferred version, and the figures in parenthesis to the eight other industries, with a half mark being given to each of the two non-nested versions for each of the eight industries.

TABLE 4.1 *Summary of preferred version for equation 4*

Cost Lags	No output function	Output function Constant	Linear	Quadratic	Total
$(0, 0, 0)$	5	0	$1(\frac{1}{2})$	$0(\frac{1}{2})$	6
$(2, 2, 2)$	$7(\frac{1}{2})$	$0(\frac{1}{2})$	$1(1)$	$2(1\frac{1}{2})$	10
$(4, 4, 2)$	$7(2\frac{1}{2})$	$2(\frac{1}{2})$	$3(\frac{1}{2})$	4	16
Total	19	2	5	6	32

NOTE: For explanation of figures in parenthesis see text.

The summary in Table 4.1 indicates that in around half of the industries (19) the preferred version does not contain output or changes in output terms. We will find later than for many of the industries where the output function is included, the impact of a rise in output on price change is not the anticipated one. The cost lags are predominantly of the four quarter lags variety, with 16 industries indicated as having lags of that length. In the industries in which the zero cost lags/no output function was preferred, the estimated coefficients on at least one of the cost change terms was statistically significant (at the 5 per cent level or better using a two-tailed t-test) in four cases out of the five.

Table 4.1 does indicate something of the differences between industries in terms of the preferred version of the price change equations with variations in the nature of the costs lags and of the output function. This variation is further reinforced when consideration is given to the estimated coefficients.

The sum of the coefficients on changes in costs of labour, of home-produced inputs and foreign-produced inputs are given in Table 4.2, and thus indicates the eventual impact on prices of changes in each of the costs. In those eight industries where there are two preferred versions, we have used the coefficients from the version with the longest cost lags, but this does not systematically raise the sum of coefficients. The outstanding feature of Table 4.2 is the nature of the coefficients on changes in labour costs. The average sum of coefficients on changes in labour costs is just over 0.03, indicating that a 1 per cent rise in labour costs leads to a 0.03 per cent rise in prices. In judging this coefficient, it must be remembered that these estimates refer to a relatively disaggregated level, and that at that level direct labour costs form around 20 per cent of total input costs. Thus a sum of coefficients on labour costs of around 0.2 could be anticipated. Our results are clearly well below that figure.[8] The sum of labour costs coefficients is negative for a lot of industries, but this can be seen as arising from random factors operating on a sum of coefficients which is close to zero, and hence with some negative and some positive sums resulting.

In Table 4.3 we have summarised the nature of the output function for those industries in which it is present in some form in the preferred version. In those industries where there are two non-nested preferred versions, we have included those which include an output function. In two industries, both non-nested preferred versions include an output function, and both forms are reported in the table, giving an element of duplication. There are four cases where the output function is a constant, and the constant is negative in two of these, indicating that in those cases price changes are lower than otherwise when output changes are positive. There are nine cases of a linear output function, and for five of these the output function has a positive value at $q = 1$ (that is when output is on its trend line). Thus at trend levels of output there is a slight tendency towards an increase in output pushing up prices rather than pulling them down. But, the largest positive effect is such that a 1 per cent rise in output would be predicted to raise prices by 0.3 per cent. Further, the value of the

TABLE 4.2 *Sum of coefficients on cost changes in preferred version of equation 4*

Industry	Labour costs	Home costs	Foreign costs	All costs
		Sum of coefficients on		
1	.235	−.275	.784	.744
2	.061	.737	−.087	.711
3	.212	.814	.176	1.202
4	.151	.322	.421	.894
5	.060	.238	.785	1.083
6	.091	.694	−.003	.782
9	−.002	.457	.109	.564
10	.066	1.182	−.101	1.147
11	.060	.797	−.083	.774
12	−.098	.741	.110	.753
13	−.027	.854	−.001	.826
14	−.076	1.151	−.036	1.039
15	.132	1.097	−.067	1.162
16	.018	.641	.080	.739
17	.059	.701	.218	.978
18	−.008	.620	.529	1.141
19	−.146	.830	.425	1.109
20	−.061	.615	.384	.938
21	.262	−.236	.853	.879
22	−.009	.742	.146	.879
23	.099	.936	.002	1.037
24	.153	.838	.113	1.104
25	−.002	.919	.312	1.229
26	−.013	.320	.488	.795
27	.022	.014	.212	.248
28	−.002	.578	.232	.808
29	−.098	1.116	−.113	.905
30	.129	.128	.279	.536
31	.008	.664	.162	.834
32	−.012	.058	.969	1.015
33	.017	.840	−.054	.803
34	.025	1.045	−.066	1.004
35	−.002	1.496	−.401	1.093
36	−.005	.856	−.026	.775
37	.006	.790	.062	.858
38	−.055	.698	.172	.865
39	−.006	.793	.010	.797
40	.001	.823	−.081	.743
41	.021	.402	.810	1.233
43	−.032	1.168	.017	1.153
Average	.031	.680	.193	.904

TABLE 4.3   *Summary of output functions in preferred versions of equation 4*

(a) *Constant*

Industry Number	σ_1
+11	.120
26	−.350
30	−.180
+41	.502

(b) *Linear*

	σ_1	σ_2	Value at $q = 1$	Eventual sign for q greater than	
+11	−1.478	1.783	0.305	+	.829
15	−3.983	3.885	−0.098	+	1.025
16	1.541	−1.413	0.128	−	1.090
+17	.533	−.931	−0.398	−	.573
+23	−1.632	1.765	0.133	+	.925
+31	.737	−.836	−0.099	−	.882
33	1.886	−1.832	0.054	−	1.029
37	2.573	−2.653	−0.080	−	.970
43	0.801	−0.627	0.184	−	1.277

(c) *Quadratic*

	σ_1	σ_2	σ_3	Value at $q = 1$	Turning point	Value of turning point
1	399.61	−792.11	392.56	.060	1.009	.030 (min)
3	−278.08	547.25	−268.69	.480	1.018	.570 (max)
+13	−1.968	4.566	−2.471	.127	.924	.141 (max)
+19	−141.86	281.74	−139.40	.480	1.011	.490 (max)
21	7.468	59.172	−31.416	.135	.942	.241 (max)
+31	6.518	−15.029	8.393	−.118	.895	−.210 (min)
32	5.570	−11.671	6.051	−.050	.964	−.091 (min)
35	26.234	−49.082	22.971	.123	1.017	.016 (min)
38	75.557	−148.67	73.090	−.020	1.157	−.044 (min)
+40	−8.921	15.866	−7.047	−.102	1.120	.009 (max)

NOTE
+ Industries where two non-nested versions are "preferred", and the non-nested versions which contain output functions are reported here.

output function changes with the level of output, and for six cases out of nine the eventual sign of the function is negative.

In ten cases, the output function is quadratic. For six of these industries, the output function takes a positive value for $q = 1$, with a negative value in the other four. In five industries the quadratic function has the expected U-shape, but has an inverted U-shape in the other five.

These results again indicate the wide differences between industries, and they also show the relevance of the use of a quadratic output function. The results in Table 4.3 indicate that for 12 of the 21 industries represented there the impact of a rise in output (relative to its trend value) is to *lower* the rate of change of prices when the level of output is near its trend value.[9] Thus, whilst output changes play a role in 21 industries (out of the 40 considered), the role is the anticipated one in only 9 cases.

The second approach is based on the idea of modelling demand changes directly. In a sense the two approaches which we have followed here are analogous to those followed under the excess demand heading – the use of output and other proxies for excess demand and the attempt to model directly excess demand in terms of demand and supply functions. It should be noted, however, that the problems of using output changes are by no means as intense as those surrounding the use of output (and related variables) as measures of excess demand. We have taken a simple view of the determinants of demand in an industry, namely that demand is a function of relative price of output of the industry compared with the general level of wholesale prices, and of aggregate income. The demand for output of industry in question can then be written as $D = D(p, p_w, Y)$ where p_w is the aggregate wholesale price level and Y some measure of aggregate demand. The price equation can be written $p = g(v).h(q, Z)$. When demand is satisfied, with output and demand equal, then we have two equations involving the two endogeneous variables at the firm level (p and q), and exogenous (to the firm) variables (p_w, v, Y and Z). In principle these equations can be solved to give $p = i(Y, p_w, v)$ and $q = j(Y, p_w, v)$ (suppressing Z which is assumed to be unchanging). Our interest is, of course, in the price equation from which a price change equation can be derived of the form:

$$\dot{p} = e_1 \dot{Y} + e_2 \dot{p}_w + e_3 \dot{v} \tag{5}$$

We can say little about the value of these coefficients e_i, apart from expecting them to be positive. In particular, there is no reason to think that e_2 or the sum of e_3's will be unity.

The alternative equation for estimation is of the general form:

$$\dot{p}_t = \alpha_0 + \alpha_1 S_{1t} + \alpha_2 S_{2t} + \alpha_3 S_{3t} + \sum_{i=1}^{n_h} \beta_i \dot{h}_{t-i} + \sum_{i=1}^{n_f} \gamma_i \dot{f}_{t-i}$$

$$+ \sum_{i=1}^{n_l} \gamma_i \dot{l}_{t-i} + \varepsilon_1 \dot{Y}_t + \varepsilon_2 \dot{p}_{wt} + u_t \tag{6}$$

An analogous procedure was followed here as with equation 4. The differences were first that the estimation technique was ordinary least squares.[10] A second difference was that an F-test was used to judge whether to proceed from a less restricted version to a more restricted version. Finally, the equation was estimated with allowance for up to fifth order serial correlation.[11] The degree of serial correlation which was allowed for was determined by the degree present in the most general version of equation 6.

A summary of the preferred versions is given in Table 4.4. As before, there are cases of non-nested versions between which we were unable to choose, and a half mark for each of these versions in the six industries in this category is recorded in parenthesis in the table. In comparison with the results for equation 4, we find that the lags on cost changes are indicated as being somewhat shorter, and demand changes are found to play a significant role in 22 industries out of the 34 for which there was a unique preferred version. Further discussion of the role of demand changes is postponed until Table 4.6 is discussed below. In the six industries where the zero cost lag/no demand version is preferred, in all cases at least one of the cost change terms is statistically significant and the correlation between actual and predicted values of price change exceeds 0.73.

TABLE 4.4 *Summary of preferred versions of equation 6*

Cost lags	No "demand" changes	"Demand" changes	Total
$(0,0,0)$	6	3(2)	9
$(2,2,2)$	$1(\frac{1}{2})$	10(1)	11
$(4,4,2)$	$5(2\frac{1}{2})$	9	14
Total	12	22	34

NOTE For explanation of figures in parenthesis see text.

In Table 4.5 we have summarised the coefficients on the cost change terms in the preferred version. As with Table 4.2, where there are two preferred versions, we have taken the results for the version with the longest lags. As anticipated, the coefficients in Table 4.5 are generally below their counterparts in Table 4.2. In those cases where the sum of coefficients is substantially out of the anticipated range of zero to unity, the estimated coefficient on the $\dot{p}_w$ term tends to compensate. For example, in industry 32 the sum of coefficients is -1.268, and the

TABLE 4.5 *Summary of coefficients on cost terms in preferred version*
of equation 6
Sum of Coefficients on

Industry no.	Labour costs	Home costs	Foreign costs	All costs
1	−.155	−.378	.410	−.123
2	−.184	.654	−.158	.312
3	.021	.316	.484	.821
4	.143	.393	.514	1.050
5	.144	−.083	.714	.775
6	−.059	−.019	−.070	−.148
9	.007	.530	.088	.625
10	.021	1.277	−.144	1.154
11	−.344	1.231	.111	.998
12	−.103	.611	.151	.659
13	−.031	.823	.173	.965
14	−.185	1.161	.010	.986
15	.177	1.076	−.076	1.177
16	.222	.026	.270	.518
17	.165	.755	.561	1.481
18	−.010	.703	.518	1.211
19	−.222	1.769	.396	1.943
20	−.293	−1.576	.558	−1.311
21	.054	.609	.320	.983
22	−.019	.802	.133	.916
23	.065	1.089	.185	1.339
24	.109	.894	.055	1.058
25	.023	1.067	.099	1.189
26	.146	.329	.368	.843
27	−.005	.908	−.109	.794
28	−.030	.314	−.008	.276
29	−.236	1.317	−.147	.934
30	.193	−.358	−.121	−.286
31	.009	.821	−.191	.639
32	−.007	−2.173	.912	−1.268
33	.039	.867	−.073	.833
34	.012	1.052	−.056	1.008
35	.076	1.267	−.288	1.055
36	−.062	.874	.026	.838
37	.105	1.036	.145	1.286
38	.024	.192	.255	.471
39	−.022	.977	−.033	.952
40	−.026	1.026	−.230	.770
41	−.042	1.359	.725	2.042
43	−.064	.171	−.180	−.073
Average	−.009	.593	.158	.742

estimated coefficient on $\dot{p}_w$ is 1.850. But in other respects the tone of these coefficients is similar to that for those reported in Table 4.2.

In Table 4.6, we have summarised the coefficients on the two demand change terms for those industries in which demand changes appear to play a significant role. These industries are divided into three groups.

TABLE 4.6   *Summary of coefficients on "demand" change terms*

Industry	Coefficient on $\dot{y}$	Coefficient on $\dot{p}_W$
1	−.077	1.069*
2	−.043	.403*
6	.180	.503*
12	.099	1.496*
16	.450*	.313
17	.238	−.801*
19	−.468	−.922
20	−.073	2.744*
28	−.011	.377*
30	.096	1.413*
31	−.182	1.010*
32	−.032	1.850*
37	−.487*	−.578
38	−.252*	.317
39	−.234*	−.262
41	.187	−1.044*
43	−.027	1.150*
4	−.029	.757*
10	.133*	1.213*
11	−.145	1.004*
13	−.001	.697*
14	.118	1.898*
26	−.163	.505*
18	.091	−.514*
21	.067	4.817*
23	.305	−.374
24	−.125	−.526*
35	−.121	−.284*

NOTE
* Statistically significant at 5 % level using one-tailed test.

For the first group of 17 industries, there are no problems in selecting the preferred version. The second group consists of the six industries for which it was not possible to discriminate between two non-nested versions, one of which contained no demand change terms and the other which did. In these cases, we have reported the coefficients from the non-nested version which contained the demand change terms. The third group of five industries arise from cases, which in terms of Figure 4.1, find that the restrictions involved in a move from D to B are not rejected whilst the other restrictions involved are rejected.

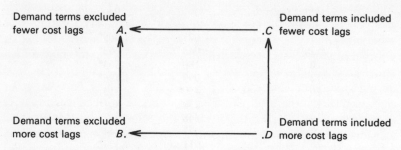

FIGURE 4.1   *Relationships between more and less general versions of equation*

In those circumstances, we have taken version D as our preferred version, but this means that the contribution of the demand change in that version is not statistically significant when compared with version B. In Table 4.6 we give the results for these industries the coefficients for the equivalent version of D.

The summary on Table 4.6 indicates clearly that changes in real income have little role to play in the determination of price changes at the industry level. In the majority of cases (17 out of the 28 reported) the coefficient on changes in real income is negative. Judged by statistical significance, the role is limited, with only seven coefficients being significant of which four are negative.

The changes in wholesale prices can be seen as representing changes in demand facing the industry or as representing the general inflationary climate. The coefficient on the price change term is predominantly positive (19 cases out of 28), and most of these coefficients are statistically significant. The average values of the coefficients on changes in wholesale prices included in Table 4.6 is 0.651 (although excluding the extreme value of over 4.8 for industry 21 lowers the mean to under 0.5), and the median values are 0.503 and 0.505.

PRICE CHANGES AND INDUSTRIAL STRUCTURE

There are a number of ways in which industrial structure has been suggested to affect price behaviour. The first is that prices change less frequently under oligopolistic situations compared with competitive conditions. The downward price rigidity of oligopolistic prices may be stressed (Sweezy, 1939), or the relative imperviness of oligopolistic prices to demand (as compared with competitive prices) (Eichner, 1973). The second is that prices of competitive (less concentrated) industries rise relative to prices of oligopolistic (more concentrated) industries during a boom, and fall relatively during a recession. This forms an element of the administered price thesis, and can be examined by regressing price changes in an industry over a specified period on level of concentration or some measure of the degree of oligopoly. The third suggestion is that prices relative to costs rise more under competitive circumstances than under an oligopolistic ones during a boom, and fall more (or rise less) during a recession. This suggestion is normally tested by regressing price changes during a specified period on appropriate cost changes and level of concentration. Most of the work in this area has been American or Canadian, though below we report on our own work in this area. The fourth suggestion is connected with earlier ones and argues that prices adjust at different rates under competitive as compared with oligopolistic conditions (Domberger, 1979). Fifthly, drawing on the distinction between price-taking and price-making behaviour, it can be argued that the price behaviour of oligopolistic industries and competitive industries could be quite different.

Before surveying previous work, as well as presenting some of our own results, two problems can be mentioned. First, there is the question as to whether the distinctions drawn between competive industries and oligopolistic industries are intended to be continuous or discontinuous relationships. In other words, is it intended that there is a sharp distinction between the behaviour of competitive prices and oligopolistic prices or that there is a gradual change in behaviour in regard to prices as the level of oligopoly/concentration changes? When the argument depends on drawing a distinction between oligopoly situations and competitive situations, then the discontinuous view would seem appropriate. But, when it is argued that (cf. p. 38 above) most, if not all, manufacturing industries (since most evidence as well as theorising draws heavily on manufacturing) are essentially oligopolistic (which here means an element of price discretion and departure from price-taking behaviour), then it makes more sense to see the effects of industrial structure in a continuous, rather than discontinuous, fashion.

Second, there is the problem of measuring the degree of oligopoly in an industry (in the "continuous" case) and of determining whether an industry is "competitive" or "oligopolistic" (in the "discontinuous" case). For the degree of oligopoly, it is usual to use measures of concentration, such as n-firm concentration ratios (that is the share of the largest n-firms in the activities of the industry, say sales or employment) or the Herfindahl index, (defined as $\sum_{i=1}^{N} s_i^2$ where s_i is share of firm i, N number of firms in industry).[12]

The discussion of evidence on price changes and industrial structure is organised along the lines of the various ways that have been postulated as outlined above. There is, inevitably, some overlap between the various routes, and also that some studies relate to more than one route. We begin with the question of price rigidity.

Means (1935) divided prices into groups based on the frequency of price changes (over the period 1926 to 1933) and compared the price changes for the ten groups (summarised in Figure One of Means 1936). It is, perhaps, not entirely surprising that during a period of low demand and general price stability, that the groups with infrequent price changes experienced a price rise *relative* to the prices of the groups whose prices changed more frequently.

Means (1972) focused on the counter-cyclical movement in those prices which he labelled as administered. The criteria for inclusion as administered was not clear-cut, but would seem to be an assessment that the price was not determined by the interplay of demand and supply nor was the price of a product which had a major input whose price was determined by demand and supply. Amongst the 50 industries which were regarded as administered price industries, Means regarded 60 per cent as generally conforming to the truncated administered price thesis, which is that such prices move up in a depression and down in a boom. The bulk of the other industries conformed to that thesis for two out of four occasions.

This contribution by Means sparked off a debate, with contributions by Stigler and Kindahl (1973), Weston *et alia* (1974), Weiss (1977). Stigler and Kindahl (1973) sought to argue that the evidence did not support the administered price thesis, though their rearrangement of the data (which they developed in Stigler and Kindahl (1970) and used by Means (1972)) indicated a significant degree of contra-cyclical price movements. For example, 19 out of 40 industries exhibited price decreases in the 1961/2 recovery, with a further 16 showing no price change.

Weston *et al.* (1974) related price increases to the level of concentration, arguing for little relationship. Weiss (1977) related the extent of price change to industrial structure. He found some evidence to favour the administered price thesis. In particular, when grouped according to administered prices or market dominated and intermediate the former rose relative to the latter during contractions and fell relatively during the recoveries. A summary of these studies is given in Sawyer (1981) pp. 140–1.

In our own investigations, we were able to relate the various measures of price rigidity to the level of concentration (measured by four-firm concentration ratio and by the Herfindahl index) for 77 UK industries over the period 1963 to 1975. We looked at discontinuous relationships by splitting the sample into above average and below average concentration industries, and comparing the measures of price rigidity for the two groups. Continuous relationships of linear and quadratic (in concentration) type were investigated. The measures of price rigidity were based on monthly price indices, similar in nature to those used in the investigations reported above.

The number of falls in the price index was found to be positively but not significantly related to concentration, whilst the number of changes bore no relationship to concentration. Some indicative results are given in Table 4.7. The view proposed by Eichner (1973) (see pp. 32–4 above) was tested by the relationship between the standard deviation of price changes and concentration. A negative but non-significant relationship was generally found, and again an indicative result is given in Table

TABLE 4.7 *Regressions relating price flexibility to level of concentration*

Dependent variable	Constant	Herfindahl index	$\bar{R}^2$	F
Number of price changes	100.401** (2.936)	−3.616 (30.020)	.0002	.0145
Number of price falls	28.754** (2.021)	27.079 (20.665)	.0224	1.7172
Standard deviation of price changes	1.590** (.167)	−1.594 (1.755)	.0103	.825
Number of observations: 77				

NOTES
** Statistically significant at 1% level.
* Statistically significant at 5% level.
ϕ Statistically significant at 10% level.
Standard errors in parenthesis.

4.7. Thus, within our sample in a generally inflationary era, there is little evidence that price rigidity is markedly influenced by industrial structure.

The second aspect concerns whether relative price movements during the course of the business cycle are influenced by the level of concentration. For 77 British manufacturing industries, we were able to test the proposition that price changes were related to concentration over specified phases of the business cycle. For this larger sample, cost and output data were not available, so the test relates to movements in relative prices irrespective of cost movements. The results for this larger sample are very similar to those obtained for a smaller sample with cost and output changes included, and reported in Table 4.8 below. We can briefly summarise the results as follows. In the first two downturns and the first upturn in our sample period there was no significant relationship between price changes and concentration (measured by the Herfindahl index). In the second upturn, a quadratic function of concentration performed statistically slightly better than a linear function, though both were statistically significant. The quadratic function indicated a U-shaped relationship; between price change and concentration, though the relationship was negative during most of the relevant range of concentration.[13] In the third downturn, the relationship was again found to be quadratic, but this time the relationship was an inverted U-shape with the relationship between price change and concentration positive through much of the relevant range.[14] These findings provide some, albeit limited, support for the administered price thesis.

The third aspect concerning the relationship between prices relative to costs and concentration can be divided into two parts. First, there are studies which have examined the relationship during defined phases of the trade cycle. The expectation for the administered price thesis would be for the prices in unconcentrated industries to move upwards (relative to costs) more than those in concentrated industries during the upswing of the cycle, and conversely during the downswing. Second, many American and Canadian studies have examined the relationship for year-to-year changes in prices and costs, paying little regard to which phase of the business cycle was operational.

The basic approach is the estimation of a regression of the form

$$\Delta p/p = a_0 + a_1 \Delta c/c + b_2 X + b_3 CR \qquad (5)$$

where Δp is change in price over the period concerned, and Δc corresponding changes in cost of inputs, X a variable relating to demand or changes in demand, and CR a measure of concentration. The problem which arises here is that it would be expected that the influence of a change in the price of inputs on price would depend on the relative importance of those inputs in production. Yet an equation such as that above imposes the same influence across all industries. Those studies which decompose the costs into different types generate rather suspect results for this reason. Some other studies use variable costs in sum, which avoids this problem. However, if firms actually determine price as a mark-up over more broadly defined costs (average 'total' costs), then the regression results will be influenced by the relationship between variable costs and 'total' costs.

One of the more recent American studies is Wilder, Williams and Singh (1977) who examine an equation of the form

$$\dot{p} = a_0 + a_1.\dot{c} + a_2.\dot{D} + a_3.CR8 + u$$

where $\dot{p}$ is annual rate of change of price, $\dot{c}$ of variable costs, $\dot{D}$ of ratio of average inventory to sales (as a negative demand proxy) and CR8 is eight-firm concentration ratio. The regression was estimated cross-section for 357 American 4-digit industries for each year from 1958 to 1972.

In their first batch of results the coefficient a_1 is consistently positive as expected and averages around 0.53 (with the low figures below 0.5 occurring in the period 1959 to 1962). The coefficient a_2 has the predicted negative sign on nine out of fourteen occasions of which three are significant at the 5 per cent level. The sign of a_3 is negative on 12 occasions of which three are significant at the 5 per cent level. The authors interpret this result as contradicting the administered price thesis. We would interpret it differently, as it indicates that in some periods concentration may have an impact on pricing behaviour. Further, the administered price thesis does not suggest that prices under concentration rise faster indefinitely, but rise relative to competitive prices during slumps. On the basis of their measure of demand, we divided the fourteen years into high demand and low demand years. The average value of a_3 in the low demand years was $-.0003$, whilst in the high demand years it was $-.013$, and the three significant and negative values of a_3 occur in high demand years. Those calculations may be suggestive of support for the administered price thesis with concentration having a more constraining influence on price rises in years of high demand than in years of low demand. There is one other problem of interpretation here. It is implicitly assumed that all industries mark-up on variable costs as measured here. If there was a broader measure of costs which was appropriate, which we will here call total costs, such that the ratio of variable to total costs varied with the level of concentration, then problems would arise. For then the coefficient on CR8 would pick up some of the effect of these differences in the importance of variable costs in determining prices.

The authors also explore whether firms respond to cost increases and cost decreases in a symmetrical manner. They conclude that "these results provide fairly strong evidence of an asymmetry in the response of price to changes in unit variable costs. The nature of this asymmetry is that a larger relative decrease in the rate of change of unit variable costs is required to obtain a given *reduction* in the rate of price change as compared with the increase in unit variable costs needed to obtain a similar *increase* in the rate of price change. The results are therefore consistent with some degree of downward price rigidity".

Lustgarten (1975) undertook a similar exercise for the slightly shorter period of 1958 to 1970 for 224 4-digit level American industries. He related the ratios of price in one year to that in the preceding year to a variety of terms of corresponding cost ratios and the level of concentration. The general conclusion was that concentration had little impact, with most of the coefficients on the concentration term in a battery of regression results being insignificant. But no attempt was made to relate the coefficients to particular phases of the business cycle.

There are a number of other studies which estimated regressions in the spirit of equation (5) above, but for periods of four to seven years. Unfortunately, estimates over those types of periods can tell us little. For the administered price thesis relates to different types of price movements in concentrated and unconcentrated industries during the different phases of the trade cycle. Those studies which use these much longer periods are testing a rather different hypothesis, namely is there any tendency for prices (or profits) in concentrated industries to change at a different pace to those in unconcentrated industries? For what they are worth we can briefly summarise these studies as follows. Weiss (1966) found some tendency for prices to rise faster in the more concentrated industries during the period 1953 to 1959 (which contained a long period of recession), followed by a negative but insignificant impact of concentration on price changes is the period 1959 to 1963. Dalton (1973) found a positive and significant impact of concentration on price change in the period 1958 to 1963. Weston *et al.* (1974) found a negative but insignificant impact for concentration on price changes during the 1958–65 period. In all these studies, cost variables were included.

Sellekaerts and Lesage (1973) use Canadian data for a range of subperiods within the time span of 1957 to 1963. They relate price change to changes in labour costs, material costs, output and the level of concentration. The impact of output changes on price changes is again found to be rather small, often statistically non-significant and negative (though during the period 1959 to 1961 changes in output often have a negative and significant coefficient in the price change equation). During the period 1957 to 1961 (and sub periods thereof), concentration (measured by the Hefindahl index, sometimes at establishment level, sometimes at enterprise level) is generally positive and significant. In the period 1963 to 1966 the effect of concentration on price changes is generally negative and non-significant, though here only establishment concentration data are used.

Our own work differs in a number of respects from that reported above.[15] It relates to British industries over sub-periods within the years 1963 to 1975. We have already described the data on prices, costs and output used above (pp. 52–4). We estimated equations of the form:

$$\Delta p_k / p_k = b_0 + b_1 \Delta c_k / c_k + b_2 \Delta q_k / q_k + f(\mathrm{CR}_k) \qquad (6)$$

where k is the industry index, c is an index of input prices, q is output and $f(\mathrm{CR}_k)$ is a function of concentration. The sub periods were defined in terms of general economic expansion or contraction. The periodisation was done by taking the reference cycles calculated by the Central Statistical Office, and published regularly in *Economic Trends*. This leads to:

Sub-period 1: downturn	1964 (4) to 1967 (1)
Sub-period 1: upturn	1967 (1) to 1969 (2)
Sub-period 3: downturn	1969 (2) to 1971 (4)
Sub-period 4: upturn	1971 (4) to 1973 (3)
Sub-period 5: downturn	1973 (4) to 1975 (3)

Single equation estimation is used since at the level of disaggregation which is used, the effect of an industry's price increase on its own cost increase is very small. Industries in our sample typically account for around 1 per cent of manufacturing output each.

In our regression estimation, we tried three variants for the function $f(\mathrm{CR}_k)$ in the equation above. These were (a) a variable which took value 1 if the concentration in the industry was above average, zero otherwise; (b) a linear function of the Herfindahl index; and (c) a quadratic function of the Herfindahl index. The continuous functions (i.e. variants (ii) and (iii)) were generally preferred statistically to the discontinuous function – variant (i).

The regression results reported in Table 4.8 relate price change during periods of downturn and upturn in economic activity to cost and output changes and to a quadratic function of the Hefindahl index.

As indicated above, similar regressions were estimated relating price change to a linear function of the Herfindahl index, and a high/low concentration dummy. The results, as far as this periodisation is concerned are not able to discriminate between the continuous and discontinuous relationships. However, the $\bar{R}^2$ is higher for the quadratic function than for either the linear or discontinuous case. For the two periods in which the quadratic function of the Herfindahl index is significant, it can be calculated that the turning point of the relationship occurs, in both cases, around 0.25, which is a value just outside the largest Herfindahl index in the sample. Thus, for upturn 2, the regression indicates that the impact of the Herfindahl index is negative throughout the range of observations, and for downturn 3 the impact is positive. Hence in two of the five periods there is some support for the

TABLE 4.8 *Regression results over stated period with price change (%) as dependent variable*

	Constant	Herfindahl index	H. I. squared	Cost change	Output change	$\bar{R}^2$	F
Downturn 1	2.457 (1.592)	11.746 (26.548)	− 68.240 (53.035)	.306* (.135)	.070 (.113)	.261	4.449**
Upturn 1	2.545 (1.947)	18.395 (23.976)	− 69.587 (47.725)	.328* (.129)	.196* (.082)	.192	3.318*
Downturn 2	10.711** (3.694)	36.200 (48.375)	− 112.808 (96.291)	.336* (.162)	.229 (.204)	.100	2.880
Upturn 2	13.216** (5.328)	− 227.868** (72.035)	401.60** (144.519)	.760** (.155)	.063 (.234)	.452	9.032**
Downturn 3	25.847** (6.697)	362.94 (93.22)	− 695.60** (186.66)	.196$^\phi$ (.115)	.011 (.254)	.304	5.256**

NOTES
Periods as defined in text.
Number of observations:40.
Symbols as in Table 4.7.
Standard errors in parenthesis.

administered price thesis in the sense that during the upturn prices appear to have risen less quickly in the more concentrated industries, and during the downturn to have risen more quickly (as compared with the less concentrated industries).

In these results, there is very little indication that output changes in an industry have any noticeable impact on price changes, which is rather in line with our earlier results. The coefficient on cost change term, whilst usually statistically significant, is generally far below unity. The constant term is generally statistically significant and positive, and this could be taken as indicating inflationary environment in which prices are generally expected to rise, lifting the inhibitions on firms from raising prices, at least to maintain their relative position, with relatively little effect coming through from differences between industries in terms of cost and output changes.

This idea advanced by Domberger (1979) that prices adjust at different rates as between competitive and concentrated industries has only been directly tested by that author. He starts from a price adjustment equation of the form:

$$(p_t - p_{t-1}) = \lambda(p_t^* - p_{t-1}) \tag{7}$$

where λ is the adjustment coefficient, p_t^* is a desired or 'target' price given by:

$$p_t^* = b_1 c_{1t} + b_2 D_t \tag{8}$$

where c_1 is costs, D an indicator of demand. These equations combine to give the price adjustment equation which can be estimated:

$$\Delta p_t = a + b_1 \Delta c_{1t} + b_2 \Delta D_t + (1 - \lambda)\Delta p_{t-1} \tag{9}$$

where $\Delta x = x_t - x_{t-1}$. This equation is estimated for each of 20 British industries over the period 1968 to 1977. We can note that this is a price adjustment equation rather than a rate of price change equation. The values of the adjustment coefficient are then related to the level of concentration (with a dummy reflecting the differences in the gestation period in engineering industries and other industries). His general finding is that the higher levels of concentration, by facilitating more effective collusion between firms, lead to faster price adjustment. Further, demand is found to have no significant impact on price adjustment.[16]

CONCLUSION

In this chapter, we have explored those approaches to price behaviour which rely, to a greater or lesser extent, on firms declaring prices at which they are prepared to trade, with prices linked to costs. Our discussion of price behaviour and industrial structure (particularly concentration) indicates a mixed bag of results. If we took the conventional view that industrial structure influences price levels but not price changes, then we could well react with a degree of surprise to the number of occasions when concentration turns up as a significant variable in price change equations. If we start from the administered price thesis, then we may find an uncomfortable number of occasions when concentration does not show up as playing a role. But, we must note that, partially as a consequence of the imprecise specification of the administered price thesis, the apparent tests of that thesis have specified the thesis is a variety of ways, which are not mutually consistent. A possible conclusion would be that there are periods of time when for a variety of reasons (including levels of demand, political circumstances) when concentrated and unconcentrated industries behave, in terms of price changes, in different ways.

Turning to the major topic of this chapter, we find considerable support for the view that price changes, relative to cost changes, are not strongly influenced by short-run variations in demand. We would expect that the long-term outlook for demand would influence prices through a number of routes. Buoyant demand, whilst having little effect on price-cost margin, would generate a larger pool of profits. The availability of profits and the buoyant demand may well lead to optimism and investment, thereby laying down the capacity with which to meet future demand. The level of capacity and capital intensity influences future unit costs, and thereby future prices (though the effect on future price-cost margins is a much more difficult question.)

In some respects, it is surprising that there has ever been a controversy over whether demand influences are an important factor with price changes. For if we look at the actual price-cost margins, then we find considerable stability. Over the period 1970 to 1978 for British manufacturing as a whole, the ratio of gross profits to sales fluctuated between 0.194 and 0.217, with the low reached in 1975, and of that observation is excluded the lowest ratio would be 0.201.[17] If we ascribe all of the variation to demand changes (which is to ignore, *inter alia*, the effects of price control, of the sharp oil price rises in 1973/74), and if we assume that demand changes have positive effects on price changes, and if the profit/sales ratio fell from its highest observed value to the lowest observed value in one year, then with costs rising at 10 per cent, the change in profit margin would only be able to reduce price inflation from 10 per cent to 6.8 per cent (and excluding the 1975 observation the fall would be to 7.8 per cent). This would be a once-and for-all decline in inflation, which would not be repeated in future years (from this source) an indeed may be offset as firms seek to restore profit margins.

5 Some Final Remarks

One of the central themes in our empirical work has been the demand on price behaviour. In Chapter 2, we argued that a sharp distinction should be drawn between competitive theories which link, via a Walrasian adjustment mechanism, price changes with the level of excess demand, and other price-making theories which indicate a link between price changes and demand changes, and often view that link is an insubstantial one. The distinction between a view which stresses the role of the *level* of excess demand and a view which stresses the role of *changes* in demand is clearly crucial in the debate over the control of inflation. Simply, the first view would indicate that low levels of excess demand would generate continuing falls in the rate of price increase (relative to cost increases), whilst the second view would point to a reduction in demand reducing the rate of inflation, but not continuing low levels of demand. Further the second view would often have doubts even about the effect of demand reductions on the pace of inflation.

In Chapter 3, we argued that there were grave difficulties surrounding the evaluation of the excess demand approach, arising from difficulties of measuring excess demand and expectations as well as the variety of formulations of the excess demand approach. Our discussions of earlier attempts to test the excess demand approach pointed to a number of crucial shortcomings which made it difficult to accept the results of those tests. Even so, despite the counter-claims of Laidler and Parkin (1975) that "it seemed to be well established that excess demand exerted an upward pressure on prices independently of changes in factor prices and hence costs", we found in line with Sylos-Labini (1979) that there was little evidence to bolster the excess demand view. Our own results for each of 40 British manufacturing industries using a variety of formulations of the excess demand approach, did not provide any indications that the excess demand approach should be taken seriously as an explanation of price changes.

Chapter 4 reviewed previous work on price change equations within an oligopolistic setting. The results of that review, taken together with those of our own empirical work, suggest that changes in the level of demand do not have any strong immediate effect on price changes. We indicated at the end of the previous chapter that demand may have longer term effects, operating through output, profits and investment. Since our evidence (and that of others) does not extend past the mid-1970s, we need to qualify our remarks on the impact of output changes to indicate that they apply only to the variations in output and demand which were experienced in years of relative prosperity. Thus, they may not apply to the very sharp falls in output experienced in Britain (especially manufacturing industry) in the period 1979 to 1981. However, casual observation would suggest that the effect of the 15 per cent fall in manufacturing output was not a dramatic one on price-cost margins (though that is consistent with a sharp fall in total profits).

If demand changes have relatively little impact on price changes (relative to cost changes), then it follows that the major impact of a fall in the level of demand will be on output and employment. The volume of profits will fall, although not by as much as they would if the price-cost margin were sensitive to demand pressures.

Our examination of the effect of demand on inflation has focused on output prices. Thus the advocates of demand reductions to control inflation will quickly point to the possible effects of demand on price of inputs (notably wages) and to indirect effects, via the exchange rate on the price of imports. The effect on input prices could arise from a combination of the effects of reduction in demand in the markets for those inputs and that of attempts by firms faced by declining demand to push the effects of that back on to the suppliers of the inputs by negotiating lower input prices.

Exploration of the effects of demand and unemployment on wage inflation has, of course, a long history. Space precludes a detailed survey.[1] We merely here note that there has been substantial empirical support for the view that workers pursue a target real wage with unemployment playing a minor and generally statistically insignificant role in the determination of wage changes (for example, Henry Sawyer and Smith (1976); Henry and Ormerod (1978); Henry (1981), Artis and Miller (1979)). Further, that those studies which have found a statistically significant role for excess demand (often proxied by unemployment) find it difficult to explain the recent experience of wage inflation.[2] For example, Parkin, Sumner and Ward (1976) find a coefficient of -1.9973 on the unemployment term in a wage change equation, implying a reduction of close to 2 per cent in wage changes for each 1 per cent rise in unemployment.[3] With an unemployment rate of 12 per cent, the level of early 1982, an expected rate of inflation of 10 per cent, their equation "predicts" wage inflation of *minus* 8 per cent, and the difference between the 6 per cent unemployment typical of the late 'seventies and 12 per cent is wage inflation which is 12 per cent lower. Thus real wages are predicted to be 12 per cent lower after one year of 12 per cent unemployment rather than 6 per cent unemployment, and to be a further 12 per cent lower for each year that the higher level of unemployment persists.

The route through the exchange rate is probably a more promising one from the point of view of those keen to establish an effect of demand on prices. This arises for a number of reasons. First, the foreign exchange market is likely to be a much closer approximation to a perfectly competitive market than markets for manufactured output and for labour. Thus, excess demand and expectational considerations may be much more important. Second, given the importance of expectational factors, the deflation of demand through fiscal or monetary channels, may lead to the belief of lower inflation and hence to the belief of higher (than otherwise) value for the exchange rate. Third, viewing the exchange rate as the relative price of domestic money and foreign money, a restriction of the growth of the domestic money supply could be seen as altering relative supplies and thereby relative prices.

It is often argued that investigations such as that reported above may inform about movements in relative prices, but say nothing about absolute prices and hence nothing about inflation. This charge has been made particularly about the administered price thesis. For example, Cox (1976) wrote that "(n)o advocate of oligopolistic inflation demonstrates how in a Walrasian general equilibrium system price increases in some markets (relative increases) raise the price level" (text in parenthesis in original). A first general comment on this is that it is not surprising that advocates of oligopolistic inflation have said nothing about what happens under general equilibrium since the latter relies on equilibrium under situations of perfect competition whilst oligopolistic inflation concerns situations of non-equilibrium under oligopoly. The second general comment is that in an economy where there are a large number of prices and price-makers, such that their decisions are not perfectly co-ordinated, then part of a general inflationary process will be movements in relative prices. At one stage, price of a given product may rise relative to other prices, and at other stages other prices rise to catch up. Where there are elements of downward price rigidity, then movements in relative prices (arising from, for example, changes in production costs) generate a general upward movement in prices. Price rises can then lead to increases in the money supply, and the creation of a general inflationary climate. Thirdly, if there are systematic movements in relative prices during the course of the trade cycle (as suggested by the administered price thesis) then that may have implications for resource allocation insofar as relative prices influence consumer behaviour. Fourthly, and most importantly, there is the question of how changes in the level of demand (particularly those induced by governments) will influence price and output changes. The administered price thesis suggests that the split between price change and output change may depend on the industrial structure. If that is correct, then the evidence on rising concentration in much of the post-war period in Britain might suggest that the response of the economy to demand changes will have changed. Further, since to a large extent one firm's price change is another firm's cost change or workers' real wage change, then the behaviour of prices at one level influences the behaviour of prices at a subsequent level when there are elements of cost-plus pricing at work.

The bulk of the evidence in Chapter 4 points to a statistically non-significant effect of demand changes on price changes. Thus we could say that as a first approximation, price changes depend on changes in input prices. There may be output change effects which through data problems, equation mis-specification etc. remain undetected. In particular, our discussion in Chapter 2 indicates that the quantitative effect of output changes on price changes is likely to be rather small, thus raising problems of detecting the presence of output change effects in regression analysis. Clearly, the smaller the true value of a coefficient, for a given value of a standard error, the more likely is it that the estimated coefficient will be judged to be not statistically significant from zero, and the greater are the changes that a negative coefficient (on output changes) will be thrown up.

The estimation of price equations at the level of individual industries (even though those used here may still involve in some sense too high a level of aggregation) serves as a forcible reminder of the disaggregated nature of the economy, and that prices are set by numerous agents. This simple observation has numerous implications for the discussion of inflation, and often appears to be overlooked in conventional discussion.

We can first observe that for the individual firm making a pricing decision the general rate of inflation is not the most relevant consideration, but changes in costs and in the prices of close substitutes are highly relevant. As far as the individual firm is concerned, rises in costs provide the impetus for price rises. But it is the actual experience of cost rises which generate price rises (in order to protect profit margins).[4] Firms which are supplying goods on long-term fixed price contract (more precisely a contract which does not allow for revision of price for cost changes) are amongst the few cases where expectations of cost changes are likely to be important. When inflation rose in the mid-1970s, many firms moved to much more frequent price changes than previously. When, in the mid-seventies there were dramatic and frequent rises in the price of coffee beans, the makers of instant coffee soon moved to very frequent price adjustments. Thus, whilst firms establish prices which are intended to last for a while and so tend to form a view of future movements in costs and prices, this should not lead to an excessive stress on expectations. It is only if there are institutional or legal restraints on price revisions that expectations covering the period during which price revisions cannot be made become important. In the expectations-augmented Phillips curve it is implicitly assumed that the nature of collective bargaining and the resulting implicit or explicit contracts effectively prevent renegotiation during the lifetime of the contract. This may be a reasonable view in that sphere, and expectations become important because of the length of the contract, often three years in the USA and generally one year in the UK. But, with some exceptions, firms are not so restricted in the pricing decisions.

The type of cases where expectations become important are likely to include cases where there are substantial costs to decision-making, where a product is made to customer-specification with a significant period of production, where long term contracts are important. These conditions would indicate that markets where expectations are important are those which are furthest removed from the auctioneer markets involving homogeneous products where competitive conditions (and hence excess demand) apply.

In general, we would argue, firms respond to the experience of cost changes rather than to the expectation of cost changes. When cost changes have occurred then unless prices rise profit margins will suffer. However, firms will pass on cost increases more quickly when they believe others are going to raise their prices. In a price-making setting, firms change their prices bearing in mind the likely reaction of their rivals (i.e. firms producing close substitutes). Thus the expectations of importance are likely to be those concerning rivals' prices. But even here those expectations are likely to be heavily conditioned by the experience of cost conditions often affecting all the firms in an industry. In sum, we can say that cost changes often provide the impetus for price changes, whilst expectations of changes in rivals prices permit prices to change.[5] In a similar way, wage earners respond to the experience of price rises by seeking to restore their real wages by raising money wages, and clearly unless they do so real wages fall.

The disaggregated view with emphasis on the *experience* of inflation rather than the *expectation* of inflation as the driving force for further inflation points to much greater difficulty in removing inflation from the economic system once it becomes ingrained. It appears much harder to change the experience of inflation than it is to change the expectation of inflation. The latter may be changeable by a government appearing determined enough to control the money supply or whatever else is thought necessary. But the former can only be changed by changing inflation itself! Further, if firms or workers have experienced cost increases or price (cost of living) increases, then failure to achieve price or wage increases has implications for profit margins and real wages.

The other aspect of disaggregation is a more technical one, that is whether it is appropriate to use aggregate price change equations. This has two aspects. The first one is that where there is a common framework for price change behaviour across industries (e.g. price changes follow cost changes) but where size of coefficients, number of lags, degree of serial correlation differ between industries. Our evidence presented in Chapter 4 would suggest that in each of these respects there are substantial differences even within manufacturing industries. It must be remembered that those prices equations are aggregations of individual firm behaviour. In light of this, any aggregate price equation relies on the relative weights of each sector remaining unchanged (and each price equation being "stable").

The second aspect arises when different sectors of the economy have different frameworks for pricing. In light of previous discussion the most important aspect of that would be the distinction between price-taking and price-making sectors. We can remark that we found very few industries where the excess demand approach appeared at all valid. But extending the picture to bring in non-manufacturing sectors could well increase the relative importance of price-taking sectors. If it is the case that the price-taking sector is of significance, then it means that the estimation of aggregate price equations should at least be segmented into the price-taking and price-making sectors. Further, it would also mean that macro-economic modelling should take cognizance of the differences between the two types of sectors.

There are two central conclusions arising out of this study. The first one relates to the need for the disaggregation of price equations to allow for differences between sectors in their price determination behaviours. The reasons for this were outlined immediately above. The conclusion applies both at the level of macro-econometric model-building and at the level of the construction of macro-economic theories. In our view, the over-aggregation of price and wage equations in macro-economic theory has overstated the ease with which inflation can be squeezed out of the system. This also arises from the second conclusion. This is the relative unimportance of demand factors in explaining price inflation. This conclusion arises from a consideration of the theories of price-making (reviewed in Chapter 2) and from the empirical work surveyed and reported in Chapters 3 and 4.

Appendix I
List of Industries Used in
Empirical Work

Our number	M.L.H. number	Description
1	211	Grain Milling
2	212	Bread, Flour, Confectionary
3	213	Biscuits
4	218	Fruit and Vegetable Products
5	219	Animal and Poultry Foods
6	229	Food Industries, n.e.s.
9	263	Lubricating Oil and Grease
10	272	Pharmaceuticals
11	313	Iron Castings
12	321	Aluminium
13	331	Agricultural Machinery
14	391	Hand tools and Implements
15	393	Bolts, Nuts, Screws
16	411	Man-made fibres
17	412	Cotton Spinning
18	413	Weaving Cotton
19	414	Woollen and Worsted
20	415	Jute
21	416	Rope, Twine & Net
22	417	Hosiery, etc.
23	419	Carpets
24	421	Narrow fabrics
25	422	Household textiles
26	432	Leather goods
27	446	Hats, Caps, Millinery
28	450	Footwear

29	461	Bricks, Refractory goods
30	462	Pottery
31	463	Glass
32	471	Timber
33	472	Furniture, Upholstery
34	473	Bedding etc.
35	489	Printing and Publishing n.e.s.
36	491	Rubber
37	492	Linoleum, etc.
38	493	Brushes and Brooms
39	494	Toys and Sports equipment
40	495	Miscellaneous Stationery goods
41	481	Paper and Board
43	381	Motor Vehicles

Appendix II
Derivation of Cost Indices

Three separate series for costs, of domestically produced inputs ("home costs"), of inputs purchased from overseas ("foreign costs") and of labour ("labour costs") were derived.

HOME COSTS

The basis for the calculation of both home and foreign costs was $A.p = c$, where A is the input–output matrix, p price of inputs vector and c the cost vector. For home costs, an expanded version of the 1968 input–output matrix was used. Firstly, the industry classification used for the input–output tables is more aggregated than the industry classification which is used in this study. Whereas in the input–output tables, 75 industries cover the manufacturing sector, the population from which the industries used in this study are drawn has 145 industries covering manufacturing industry. In many cases there is a one-to-one correspondence between input–output industries and those we use. But at the other extreme one input–output industry contains six Census of Production industries. Where one of the industries in our study was only part of an input–output industry, the latter industry was disaggregated in respect of the major inputs by reference to information contained in the report of the Census of Production for 1968. Major inputs were those accounting for more than 5% of costs. In the case of minor inputs, the same input–output ratio was assumed to operate for all the Census of Production industries within the input–output industry.

The second expansion of the input–output table occurred on the input side. Outside of manufacturing, there is a high degree of aggregation within the input–output table. Where an industry makes major purchases from an industry which is highly aggregated an attempt was made to disaggregate. This particularly applied where purchases from agriculture were concerned, and the particular products from agriculture were identified and price indices obtained for them.

For inputs purchased from other manufacturing industries and from mining and quarrying industries the wholesale price indices were used as the input prices. In many cases, the wholesale price index for an individual industry was available and in that case, it was used. In some cases, the input–output industry had a number of component MLH industries for which price indices were available. In those cases, the indices for the component industries were combined using as weights the sales of the component industries. In other cases, indices for individual industries were not available, and the index for a higher level of aggregation was used.

For agriculture (input–output 1), and forestry and fishing (2), attempts were made to identify the actual products which were purchased from agriculture by each industry, and then separate indices obtained for those products. Information from the 1968 Census of Production was mainly used.

The remaining inputs from domestic suppliers were dealt with in the following manner:

81. Construction:	Cost index of new construction in housing and construction statistics.
82. Gas	Industrial users index in digest of energy statistics.
83. Electricity	Industrial users index in digest of energy statistics.
84. Water supply:	Unit value series derived from statistics published by Chartered Institute of Public Finance Accountancy.
85, 86, 87, 88:	Transport National Income and Expenditure Blue Book and Communication.
89, 90.	Distribution Trade and Miscellaneous Services – see note below.

Let W_i be the weights for an input price index for miscellaneous services

W_i^* be the weights for an input price index for distribution.

Let P_s and P_d be unknown price indices for services and distribution. Then

$$\sum W_i P_i + W_d Pd + W_s P_s = P_s$$
$$i \neq d, s$$
$$\sum W_i^* P_i + W_d^* P_d + W_s^* P_s = P_d$$

so that

$$\begin{bmatrix} P_s \\ P_d \end{bmatrix} = \begin{bmatrix} 1 - W_s & -W_d \\ -W_s^* & 1 - W_d^* \end{bmatrix} \begin{bmatrix} \sum_i W_i P_i \\ \sum_i W_i^* P_i \end{bmatrix}$$

The cost indices were derived on a quarterly basis with $1963 = 100$ using 1968 weights. When only annual data were available for the input costs, these were put onto a quarterly basis in the following manner:

Price in qtr. $1 = (1.5)P_{-1} + (2.5)P$
$2 = (0.5)P_{-1} + (3.5)P$
$3 = (3.5)P + (0.5)P_{+1}$
$4 = (2.5)P + (1.5)P_{+1}$

where P_{-1} is price in previous years, P in current year and P_{+1} in subsequent year.

FOREIGN COSTS

The manner of constructing the foreign costs series was basically the same as that for home costs, but the number of groups into which the inputs are placed was much less. The input–output table which was used in this context was Table C of the 1968 input–output Tables which provides for each industry the imported inputs in that year.

The Department of Trade and Industry provided import cost series for 11 groupings.

For those industries which made substantial purchases of agricultural imports (input–output), attempts were made to see whether there were one or two main agricultural products which the industry used, and if so to collect information on the prices of those products.

LABOUR COSTS

The labour costs series is based on the earnings of manual workers, and makes the implicit assumption that the costs of manual and non-manual labour moves together. The starting point is the earnings in money terms of the five groups of manual workers (men, boys, women (full-time), women (part-time) and girls). These figures were available bi-annually (April and October) up to (and including) 1969, annually (October) thereafter. The quarterly figures were obtained by interpolation, using the monthly index of earnings for all manufacturing.[1]

In order to obtain labour costs, employers national insurance contributions were added to the earnings figures. The overall costs were then obtained by weighting these labour costs by current employment weights.

The overall cost index was then obtained by taking a weighted average of home costs, foreign costs and unit labour costs, where the weights were based on the costs proportions given in the 1968 Input–Output Tables.

Notes

1 INFLATION, PRICING AND PROFITS

1. There are numerous references on the nature of monetarism and the Keynesian-monetarist debate, for example, Burrows (1979), Morgan (1978), Laidler (1981), Mayer (1978), Purvis (1980), Vane and Thompson (1979).
2. For further discussion on the role of price rigidity in the Keynesian approach, see Sawyer (1982a) Chapter 3.
3. This is usually described under the heading of the "surprise" supply function, on which see, for example, Lucas and Rapping (1969), Lucas (1973), Sargent (1973), Sargent (1979).
4. See, for example, Bailey (1956), Foster (1976).
5. The "shoe-leather" argument is usually developed assuming a zero (or at least constant) rate of interest on money. The costs would be reduced if the rate of interest on money rose with the rate of inflation. The extent to which current accounts with clearing banks pay interest (even if it is only inputed and offset against service charges) reduces these costs.
6. It is likely, in practice, to be difficult to identify any one group as triggering off an inflationary cycle. Further, there will be struggles over income shares within the four main groups which have been identified.

2 THEORIES OF PRICING

1. The discussion below is undertaken for the specific purpose of deriving a price and then a price change equation. Thus many aspect of these theories are neglected here; for fuller discussion see, for example, Sawyer (1979).
2. Homogeneous product in any context will lead to the conclusion of identical prices across firms. But under oligopoly conditions, even with Cournot-type behaviour, firms charge a price above marginal cost and earn supernormal profits through output restriction. This requires blockaded entry for otherwise firms would enter to erode the supernormal profits.
3. From $\pi = p \cdot q\ (x_1, x_2, \ldots x_n) - \sum_{i=1}^{n} r_i x_i$, profit maximisation conditions include $\dfrac{\partial q}{\partial x_i} = r_i$, i.e. marginal product of factor i equals its price r_i. This general formulation reinforced the point made later in the text that factors are not distinguished from each other. Out of equilibrium, factor payments would not exactly add up to the revenue of the firm, leaving some factor with a residual (positive or negative).

4. There are two crucial problems. The first is the question of whether payment to each factor according to marginal product would exhaust the total product – the adding-up problem. This is "solved" by the assumption that at least over a range of output there is constant returns to scale, and in equilibrium firms will operate in that range. The second relates to the use of the marginal productivity theory as a theory of aggregate income distribution, where problems of the measurement of capital arise. Specifically, the question arises from the re-switching literature as to whether it is possible to derive a downward-sloping demand for aggregate capital as a function of the rate of profit. For further discussion, see Garegnani (1970, 1978), Harcourt (1975).
5. Discussion with Brian Henry on this approach is gratefully acknowledged; see also Henry (1981).
6. In the original article, Parkin used dX_i/dt rather than ΔX_i, which mixes the use of discrete time periods with continuous time.
7. The advantage of using a logarithmic function in (1) is evident here. For log $x_t - \log x_{t-1} = \log x_t/x_{t-1} = \log (1 + (x_t - x_{t-1})/x_{t-1}) \doteq (x_t - x_{t-1})/x_{t-1}$.
8. Equation (5) also indicates that changes in excess demand and changes in price are negatively related, which is rather counter-intuitive. But this arises because changes in excess demand do not cause price changes, but price changes are used to change excess demand.
9. The lag of price changes behind excess demand is introduced with the move into discrete time. The variable $\dot{p}_{it}$ is the change in price from period $t-1$ to period t, and thus it is more reasonable to postulate that the level of excess demand in period $t-1$ influences that change rather than the level in period t.

3 EXCESS DEMAND, EXPECTATIONS AND PRICE CHANGES

1. For further details, see Board of Trade Journal, 21 Feb. 1969.
2. For further discussion, see Aaronovitch and Sawyer (1975) pp. 60–62.
3. This point was raised in the context of the labour market and the Phillips' curve by Holmes and Smyth (1970).
4. It is assumed that demand (D) depends on p_i/p and supply (S) on c/p_i, so that equilibrium is given by $D(p_i/p) = S(c/p_i)$. The previous equilibrium output will be maintained if p_i/p and c/p_i are unchanged in equilibrium which will be the case when p, c and p_i change at the same rate.
5. For further discussion, see Sawyer (1982c).
6. For further discussion, see Wallis (1980).
7. Unfortunately, Laidler and Parkin do not give any reference in their bibliography to McCallum (1974). The references provided there for McCallum (1973) and (1975) do not undertake relevant estimation.
8. The price term is wholesale 'factory gate' price excluding any indirect taxes on output (e.g. purchase tax, value added tax), but does include the effects of taxes on inputs such as excise duty. This is important in a number of industries where changes in excise duty dominate price changes (e.g. spirits). The introduction of value added tax in April 1973 substituted an output tax for part of the input tax (excise duty) which is reflected in a sharp drop in the price indices for industries where excise duty is important. Such industries have been excluded from our sample. There is a small effect on the aggregate

wholesale price index, and we have adjusted that index after April 1973 to take account of the tax changes.

9. Apart from the reasons given above (p. 54) for relating $\dot{p}_{it}$ to excess demand at time $t-1$, there are econometric reasons for doing so. If excess demand at time t were used, then terms involving p_{it} would appear on the right-hand side. Whilst we can treat p_{it-1} as predetermined for period t, we cannot reasonably make that assumption so far as p_{it} is concerned. We would then be 'explaining' p_{it} relative to p_{it-1} in terms of p_{it} relative to p_{wt} and c_{it}.

4 COST CHANGES, DEMAND CHANGES AND PRICE CHANGES

1. There is also the question as to whether cost changes have any direct effect on price changes. Many would see that as a question which has the obvious answer of Yes. But in the context of excess demand approach (especially the first and fourth variants estimated in the previous chapter) cost changes do not have a direct impact, but work via effect on excess demand. For products which are traded internationally it could be argued through the "law of one price" that producers in a small economy (i.e. producers who have to operate as price-takers) have no discretion over price charged. Hence changes in domestic prices are dictated by changes in world prices.

2. Since production takes time, the question arises of to which notion of costs the firm applies the mark-up. Firms could use replacement cost, and hence use the current price of inputs in determining costs. Another possibility is that firms could use historic costs, that is use the price actually paid for inputs embodied in current output. These represent, in a sense, the two extreme possibilities, and firms could use some amalgam. Coutts, Godley and Nordhaus try replacement, historic costs and an average of those two costs as the basis for their normalised cost calculations, and in general prefer the average measure.

3. These figures relate to, in the notation of Coutts, Godley and Nordhaus (1978) R_u^2 which "allows for the use of first or second order error process, in the sense that we avoid indicating a high degree of fit which may be based not on the deterministic part of the regression but mainly on the presence of autocorrelation of errors". Essentially in a regression of the form $\Delta \ln p_t = a_0 + a_1 \Delta \ln \hat{p}_t + u_t$ where u_t is autocorrelated, the calculation of R_u^2 is based on the variance of u_t, rather than on the variance e_t in the autoregressive process $u_t = p_0 + p_1 u_{t-1} + p_2 u_{t-2} + e_t$.

4. They also try equations which relate the price level to the level of normalised price and of output relative to trend. For full discussion, see Coutts, Godley and Nordhaus (1978) p. 64–72.

5. In terms of equation 1, half were estimated with a_1 constrained at unity and half with a_1 unconstrained. The demand terms were included either in current terms only or with current and three lagged terms. The level of price was related to the level of demand, and changes in price level to level of demand as well as to changes in demand. This provides 12 versions.

6. We did not think it worthwhile to seek to arrive at a decision between the non-nested version.

7. We did some experimentation on estimation with allowance for serial correlation, but soon discovered that the amount of computer time required would be very high (something over 24 hours of computer time for the most general version). Further the specification tests indicated no need for such estimation.

8. It might be thought that this results from our use of only up to two lags on labour costs. However, in other work, we have used up to six lags without any difference to the tone of our results.

9. The results for the two industries which appear twice in Table 4.3 are qualitatively the same whichever version is used.

10. The extent of any feedback of price rise in one industry on its costs within one quarter was judged to be insignificant and hence ignored. Remember that each industry considered here constitutes around 1 per cent of manufacturing industry. We are dealing with wholesale prices, which tend to affect retail prices and thereby wages with considerable lags.

11. In contrast to the instrumental variable estimation of equation 3, considerable serial correlation is indicated here.

12. For discussion of these and other measures of concentration see text books on industrial economics, e.g. Sawyer (1981).

13. The turning point of the U-shaped curve occurring where the Herfindahl index equals 0.262.

14. The turning point this time occurring for Herfindahl index value of 0.198.

15. For further discussion and results, see Aaronovitch and Sawyer (1981).

16. See, however, the debate between Domberger (1981) and Winters (1981).

17. In these calculations, gross profits equal net output minus wages and salaries.

5 SOME FINAL REMARKS

1. For a brief survey by the present author see Sawyer (1982a) Chapter Seven, and for a critique of the Phillips curve see Sawyer (1982c). The survey by Laidler and Parkin (1975) supports the view that excess demand for labour and inflationary expectations explain wage inflation. The survey by Artis and Miller (1979) presents a different view.

2. Space precludes further discussion of the model used by Parkin, Sumner and Ward (1976). On this see Sawyer (1982c).

3. The model used in the wage change analogue of the Parkin (1975) price equation discussed in Chapter Two. Many of our criticisms expressed there apply to the wage change equation. It should be noted that a statistically significant coefficient on unemployment arises only in a restricted version. In an unrestricted estimate the coefficient is not statistically significant with a t-value of 0.70. Note also that Godley (1977) indicates restrictions only just escape rejection by the data.

4. But under profit maximisation conditions, if the elasticity of demand, degree of effective collusion etc. do not change neither will the profit maximising mark-up.

5. This is not intended to rule out a general "profits-push", in which there is a concerted attempt to raise profit margins, as an initiation factor in an inflationary process.

APPENDIX II

1. The method used was as follows. If the over-all manufacturing earnings index (monthly values $M_1, M_2, \ldots, M_1$) grows at six-month rate of h, whilst earrings in the industry change at rate g, we calculate $r = ((1+g)/(1+h))^{1/6}$ for each category of the industry's workers. Then if $E_{i,q}$ are the required quarterly values of earnings, then

$$E_{i,2} = (1/3)E_{i,\text{April}} \left(1 + r.M_5/M_4 + r^2.M_6/M_4\right)$$
$$E_{i,3} = (1/3)E_{i,\text{April}} \left(r^3 M_7/M_4 + r^4 M_8/M_4 + r^5.M_9/M_4\right)$$

and similarly for quarters 4 and 1 using October instead of April values.

Bibliography

Aaronovitch, S. and Sawyer, M. (1975), *Big Business: Theoretical and Empirical Aspects of Concentration and Mergers in the United Kingdom*, (Macmillan, 1975).

Aaronovitch, S., and Sawyer, M., (1981), "Price Change and Oligopoly", *Journal of Industrial Economics*, vol. 30.

Andrews, P. (1949), *Manufacturing Business* (Macmillan, 1949).

Andrews, P. (1964), *On Competition in Economic Theory* (Macmillan, 1964).

Arrow, K. (1959), "Towards a Theory of Price Adjustment" in M. Abramovitz (ed.) *The Allocation of Economic Resources* (Stanford University Press, 1959).

Artis, M. and Miller, M. (1979), "Inflation, Real Wages and the Terms of Trade", in J. K. Bowers (ed.) *Inflation, Development and Integration*, (Leeds University Press, 1979).

Bailey, M. (1956), "The Welfare Cost of Inflationary Finance", *Journal of Political Economy*, vol. 64.

Bain, J. S. (1956), *Barriers to New Competition* (Harvard University Press, 1956).

Barro, R. and Grossman, H. (1976), *Money, Employment and Inflation* (Cambridge University Press, 1976).

Baumol, W. (1959), *Business Behaviour, Value and Growth* (Macmillan, 1959).

Beals, R. E. (1975), "Concentrated Industries, Administered Prices and Inflation: A Survey of Recent Empirical Research", paper prepared for the Council on Wage and Price Stability, Washington, 1975.

Brechling, F. (1972), "Some Empirical Evidence on the Effectiveness of Price and Income Policies", in J. M. Parkin and M. Sumner (1972).

Breusch, R. S. and Godfrey, L. G., (1981), "A Review of Recent Work on Testing for Autocorrelation in Dynamic Economic Models", in Currie, Nobay and Peel (1981).

Burrows, P., (1979), "The Government Budget Constraint and the Monetarist Keynesian Debate", in S. T. Cook and P.M. Jackson (eds), *Current Issues in Fiscal Policy* (Martın Robertson, 1979).

Chatterji, M. and Wickens, M. (1981), "Verdoern's Law – the Externalities Hypothesis and Economic Growth in the U.K.", in Currie, Nobay and Peel (1981).

Clower, R. (1965), "The Keynesian Counter-Revolution: A Theoretical Appraisal", in F. Hahn and F. Brechling (eds) *The Theory of Interest Rates* (Macmillan, 1965).

Coutts, K. Godley, W. and Nordhaus, W. (1978), *Industrial Pricing in the United Kingdom* (Cambridge University Press, 1978).

Cowling, K. (1982), *Monopoly Capitalism* (Macmillan, 1982).

Cox, C. C., (1976), Review of S. Lustgarten *Industrial Concentration and Inflation* (A.E.I., Washington, 1975), *Journal of Money Credit at Banking*, vol. 8.

Currie, D., Nobay, R. and Peel, D. (1981) (eds) *Macroeconomic Analysis*, (Croom Helm, 1981).

Cyert, R. M. and March, J. G., (1963), *A Behavioural Theory of the Firm*, (Prentice-Hall, 1963).

Dalton, J. A. (1973), "Administered Inflation and Business Pricing: Another Look", *Review of Economics and Statistics*, vol. 55.

Dobb, M. (1973), *Theories of Value and Distribution Since Adam Smith*, (Cambridge University Press, 1973).

Domberger, S. (1979), "Price Adjustment and Market Structure", *Economic Journal*, vol. 89.

Domberger, S. (1981), "Price Adjustment and Market Structure: A Reply", *Economic Journal*, vol. 91.

Eckstein, O. and Fromm, G. (1968), "The Price Equation", *American Economic Review*, vol. 58.

Eichner, A. (1973), A Theory of the Determination of the Mark-up under Oligopoly", *Economic Journal*, vol. 83.

Eichner, A. (1976), *The Megocorp and Oligopoly: Micro Foundations of Macro Dynamics* (Cambridge University Press, 1976).

Foster, J. (1976), "The Redistributive Effects of Inflations – Questions and Answers", *Scottish Journal of Political Economy*, vol. 23.

Friedman, M. (1970), "A Theoretical Framework for Monetary Analysis", *Journal of Political Economy*, vol. 78.

Garegnani, P. (1970), "Heterogenous Capital, the Production Function and the Theory of Distribution", *Review of Economic Studies*, vol. 37.

Garegnani, P. (1978), "Notes on Consumption, Investment and Effective Demand I", *Cambridge Journal of Economics*, vol. 2.

Geary, R. C. (1970), "Relative Efficiency of Count of Sign Changes for Assessing Residual Autoregression in Least Squares Regression", *Biometrika*, vol. 57.

Godfrey, L. G. (1972), "Some Comments on the Estimation of the Lipsey-Parkin Inflation Model" in Parkin and Sumner (1972).

Godley, W. and Nordhaus, W. (1972), "Pricing in the Trade Cycle", *Economic Journal*, vol. 82.

Godley, W. A. (1977), "Inflation in the United Kingdom", in L. B. Krause and W. S. Salant (eds), *Worldwide Inflation: Theory and Experience* (Brookings Institute, Washington, 1977).

Hall, R. L. and Hitch, C. J. (1939), "Price Theory and Business Behaviour", *Oxford Economic Papers*.

Harcourt, G. C. (1975), "The Cambridge Controversies: The Afterglow" in Parkin and Nobay (1975).

Harcourt, G. and Kenyon, P. (1976), "Pricing and the Investment Decision", *Kyklos*, vol. 29.

Harris, D. (1978), *Capital Accumulation and Income Distribution* (Stanford University Press, 1978).

Hay, D. and Morris, D. (1979), *Industrial Economics* (Oxford University Press, 1979).

Henry, S. G. B. (1981), "Incomes Policy and Aggregate Pay" in J. Fallick, and R. F. Elliot (eds) *Incomes Policy, Inflation and Relative Pay*, (Allen & Unwin, 1981).

Henry, S. G. B. and Ormerod, P. (1978), "Incomes Policies and Wage Inflation: Empirical Evidence for the U.K., 1961–1977", *National Institute Economic Review*, no. 85.

Henry, S. G. B., Sawyer, M. C. and Smith, P. (1976), "Models of Inflation in the United Kingdom", *National Institute Economic Review*, no. 77.

Holmes, J. and Smyth, D. J. (1970), "The Relationship Between Unemployment and Excess Demand for Labour: an Examination of the Theory of the Phillips' Curve", *Economica*, vol. 37.

Howard, M. (1983), *Theories of Profit* (Macmillan, 1983).

Kalecki, M. (1971), *Selected Essays on the Dynamics of the Capitalist Economy*, (Cambridge University Press, 1971).

Keynes, J. (1930), *A Treatise on Money* (Macmillan, 1930).

Kmenta, J. (1971), *Elements of Econometrics* (Collier-Macmillan, 1971).

Laidler, D. (1973), "The Influence of Money on Real Income and Inflation: a Simple Model with Some Empirical Tests for the United States, 1953–72", *Manchester School*, vol. 41.

Laidler, D. (1981), "Monetarism: An Interpretation and An Assessment", *Economic Journal*, vol. 91.

Laidler, D. and Parkin, J. M. (1975), "Inflation: A Survey", *Economic Journal*, vol. 85.

Leijonhufvud, A. (1967), "Keynes and the Keynesians: A suggested Interpretation", *American Economic Review*, vol. 57.

Lucas, R. (1973), "Some International Evidence on Output-Inflation Trade Offs", *American Economic Review*, vol. 63.

Lucas, R. and Rapping, L. (1969), "Real Wages, Employment and Inflation", *Journal of Political Economy* vol. 77.

Lustgarten, S. (1975), "Administered Inflation: a Reappraisal, *Economic Inquiry*, vol. 13.

McCallum, B. (1970), "The Effect of Demand on Prices in British Manufacturing Industry: Another View", *Review of Economic Studies*, vol. 37.

McCallum, B. T. (1973), "Friedman's Missing Equation: Another Approach", *Manchester School*, vol. 41.

McCallum, B. T. (1975), "Rational Expectations and the Natural Rate Hypothesis: Some Evidence for the United Kingdom", *Manchester School*, vol. 43.

Machlup, F. (1967), "Theories of the Firm: Marginalist, Behavioural, Managerial", *American Economic Review*, vol. 57.

Maddala, G. S. (1977), *Econometrics* (McGraw-Hill, 1977).

Mayer, T. (1978), *The Structure of Monetarism* (Norton, New York, 1978).

Means, G. C. (1935), "Industrial Prices and their Relative Inflexibility", (US Senate Document 13, 74th Congress, 1st Session, Washington, 1935).

Means, G. C. (1936), "Notes on Inflexible Prices", *American Economic Review*, vol. 26.

Means, G. C. (1972), "The Administered Price Thesis Reconfirmed", *American Economic Review*, vol. 62.

Meek, R. (1977), *Smith, Marx and After* (Chapman & Hall, 1977).

Modigliani, M. (1958), "New Developments on the Oligopoly Front", *Journal of Political Economy*, vol. 66.

Modigliani, M. (1977), "The Monetarist Controversy or Should We Foresake Stabilization Policies?," *American Economic Review*, vol. 67.

Moore, B., (1979), "Monetary Factors", in A. Eichner (ed.), *A Guide to Post-Keynesian Economics* (Macmillan, 1979).

Morgan, B. (1978), *Monetarists and Keynesians – Their Contribution to Monetary Theory* (Macmillan, 1978).

Muth, J. F. (1961), "Rational Expectations and the Theory of Price Movements", *Econometrica*, vol. 29.

Neild, R. (1963), *Pricing and Employment in the Trade Cycle* (Cambridge University Press, 1963).

Okun, A. (1981), *Prices and Quantities: A Macroeconomic Analysis* (Blackwell, 1981).

Parkin, J. M. (1975), "The Causes of Inflation: Recent Contributions and Current Controversies", in M. Parkin and A. Nobay (eds) *Current Economic Problems* (Cambridge University Press, 1975).

Parkin, J. M. (1977), "Inflation in the United Kingdom: a Comment on Godley", in L. B. Krause and W. S. Salant (eds), *Worldwide Inflation*, (Brookings Institution, Washington 1977).

Parkin, J. M. and Sumner, M. (1972) (eds), *Incomes Policy and Inflation*, (Manchester University Press, 1972).

Parkin, J. M., Sumner, M. and Ward, R. (1976), "The Effect of Excess Demand, Generalised Expectations and Wage-Price Controls on Wage Inflation in the UK", in K. Brunner, and A. Meltzer (eds) *The Economics of Wage and Price Controls* (Brookings Institute, 1976).

Purvis, D. (1980), "Monetarism – A Review", *Canadian Journal of Economics*, vol. 13.

Rowthorn, R. (1977), "Conflict, Inflation and Money", *Cambridge Journal of Economics*, vol. 1.

Rushdy, F. and Lund, P. J. (1967), "The Effect of Demand on Prices in British Manufacturing Industry", *Review of Economic Studies*, vol. 33.

Sargan, J. D. (1964), "Wages and Prices in the United Kingdom: a study in Econometric methodology", in P. E. Hart, G. Mills, and J. K. Whittaker (eds), *Econometric Analysis for National Economic Planning* (Butterworth, 1964).

Sargent, T. J. (1973), "Rational Expectations, the Real Rate of Interest and the National Rate of Unemployment", *Brookings Papers on Economic Activity*, vol. 2.

Sargent, T. J. (1979), *Macroeconomic Theory* (Academic Press, 1979).

Sawyer, M. (1979), *Theories of the Firm* (Weidenfeld & Nicolson, 1979).

Sawyer, M. (1981), *Economics of Firms and Industries* (Croom Helm, 1981).

Sawyer, M. (1982a), *Macroeconomics in Question* (Wheatsheaf Books, 1982).

Sawyer, M. (1982b), "Collective Bargaining, Oligopoly and Macroeconomics", *Oxford Economic Papers*, vol. 34.

Sawyer, M. (1982c), "The Non-Keynesian Nature of the Phillips' Curve", *University of York Discussion Paper*, no. 82.

Sellekaerts, W. and Lesage, R. (1973), "A Reformulation and Empirical Validation of the Administered Price Inflation Hypothesis: The Canadian Case", *Southern Economic Journal*, vol. 39.

Shephard, R. W. (1970), *Theory of Cost and Production Functions* (Princeton University Press, 1970).

Silberston, A. (1970), "Price Behaviour of Firms", *Economic Journal*, vol. 80.

Simon, H. A. (1959), "Theories of Decision Making in Economics and Behavioural Science", *American Review Economic*, vol. 49.

Solow, R. (1969), *Price Expectations and the Behaviour of the Price Level*, (Manchester University Press, 1969).

Spence, A. M. (1977), "Entry, Capacity, Investment and Oligopolistic Pricing", *Bell Journal of Economics*, vol. 8.

Sraffa, P. (1960), *Production of Commodities by Means of Commodities* (Cambridge University Press, 1960).

Steadman, I. (1981), "Ricardo, Marx, Sraffa" in I. Steadman and others *The Value Controversy* (Verso Books, 1981).

Stigler, G. J. and Kindahl, J. K. (1970) *The Behaviour of Industrial Prices*, (National Bureau for Economic Research, New York, 1970).

Stigler, G. J. and Kindahl, J. K. (1973) "Industrial Prices as Administered by Dr. Means", *American Economic Review*, vol. 63.

Sweezy, P. (1939), "Demand under Conditions of Oligopoly", *Journal of Political Economy*, vol. 47.

Sylos-Labini, P. (1962), *Oligopoly and Technical Progress* (Harvard University Press, 1962).

Sylos-Labini, P. (1979), "Review Article: Industrial Pricing in the United Kingdom", *Cambridge Journal of Economics*, vol. 3.

Tobin, J. (1972), "Inflation and Unemployment", *American Economic Review*, vol. 62.

Vane, H. J. and Thompson, J. L. (1979), *Monetarism: Theory, Evidence and Policy*, (Martin Robertson, 1979).

Wallis, K. (1980), "Econometric Implications of the Rational Expectations Hypothesis", *Econometrica*, vol. 48.

Walras, L. (1954), *Elements of Pure Economics*, (trans. by W. Jaffe), (Irwin, Homewood, Illinois, 1954).

Weiss, L. W. (1966), "Business Pricing Policies and Inflation Reconsidered", *Journal of Political Economy*, vol. 74.

Weiss, L. W. (1977), "Stigler, Kindahl and Means on Administered Prices", *American Economic Review*, vol. 67.

Weston, J. F., Lustgarten, S. and Grottke, N. (1974), "The Administered Price Thesis Denied: Note", *American Economic Review*, vol. 64.

Wilder, R., Williams, C. and Singh, D. (1977), "The Price Equation: a Cross-section Approach", *American Economic Review*, vol. 67.

Winters, D. (1981), "Price Adjustment and Market Structure: a Comment", *Economic* Journal, vol. 91.

Index

The terms prices, price change are not indexed. The specific aspects of prices and price-changes are separately indexed (e.g. administered prices).